How to Teach the Old Testament to Christians

HOW TO

Teach the Old Testament to Christians

Discover How to Unpack

All of Scripture

for Today's Believers

T. J. Betts

THOM S. RAINER, SERIES EDITOR

TYNDALE
MOMENTUM®

A Tyndale nonfiction imprint

Visit Tyndale online at tyndale.com.

Visit Tyndale Momentum online at tyndalemomentum.com.

Tyndale, Tyndale's quill logo, *Tyndale Momentum*, and the Tyndale Momentum logo are registered trademarks of Tyndale House Ministries. Tyndale Momentum is a nonfiction imprint of Tyndale House Publishers, Carol Stream, Illinois.

How to Teach the Old Testament to Christians: Discover How to Unpack All of Scripture for Today's Believers

For information about special discounts for bulk purchases, please contact Tyndale House Publishers at csresponse@tyndale.com, or call 1-855-277-9400.

Library of Congress Cataloging-in-Publication Data

A catalog record for this book is available from the Library of Congress.

ISBN 978-1-4964-7388-2

Printed in the United States of America

29 28 27 26 25 24 23
7   6   5   4   3   2   1

Contents

Preface

THE INTENTION OF THIS SMALL BOOK is to help Bible teachers preach and teach the Old Testament in the local church, to help Christians understand its historical and theological context, and to interpret the Old Testament through the life, death, burial, resurrection, and ascension of Jesus Christ.

The largest portion of the book covers what the Old Testament is and why we should teach it in the church today. The reason for this is simple. I'm convinced that only when we have the right motivation to do something will we do it with fervor and diligence.

When we correctly understand what the Old Testament is and why the church desperately needs to know its contents, we will appreciate the privilege and experience the joy of preparing and teaching it to our brothers and sisters in Christ.

I guarantee you will be blessed by significantly incorporating the Old Testament as part of your ongoing ministry. Those you disciple who deeply desire to grow in their knowledge of Christ and live according to his precepts will forever be grateful for your efforts.

What Is the Old Testament?

Before addressing the question of why believers should study, preach, and teach the Old Testament, it's fitting to first answer the question "What is the Old Testament?" The answer may seem obvious, but it provides a foundation for everything else.

The Scriptures

What Christians today call the Old Testament, Jesus and the New Testament writers referred to as "the Scriptures" or "Scripture."

For instance, quoting Psalm 118:22-23, Jesus said, "Didn't you ever read this in the Scriptures? 'The stone that the builders rejected has now become the cornerstone. This is the LORD's doing, and it is wonderful to see'" (Matthew 21:42).

Also, in Romans 4:3, referring to Genesis 15:6, the apostle Paul writes, "The Scriptures tell us, 'Abraham believed God, and God counted him as righteous because of his faith.'"

These are just a couple of the approximately fifty times the expressions "the Scriptures" or "Scripture" in the New Testament refer to the Old Testament. Writing to Timothy, Paul also said, "All Scripture is inspired by God" (2 Timothy 3:16).

From these passages, we can see that the Old Testament is the eternal, inerrant, authoritative Word of God (Psalm 119:160; Isaiah 40:6-8; 1 Peter 1:24-25). It was the Bible that both Jesus and the early church used.

Three sections

In New Testament times, believers understood the Old Testament to have three sections: the Law, the Prophets, and the Writings. The Law contains the first five books: Genesis, Exodus, Leviticus, Numbers, and Deuteronomy.

The section called the Prophets has two parts, the Former Prophets and the Latter Prophets. The books of the Former Prophets are Joshua, Judges, Samuel, and Kings, and the books of the Latter Prophets are Isaiah, Jeremiah, Ezekiel and the Twelve (Hosea, Joel, Amos, Obadiah, Jonah, Micah, Nahum, Habakkuk, Zephaniah, Haggai, Zechariah, and Malachi), sometimes called the Minor Prophets today—because these books are short compared to the other books of the Prophets, not because they are less important or have less of an impact.

The books contained in the Writings are Psalms, Proverbs, Job, Song of Songs, Ruth, Lamentations, Ecclesiastes, Esther, Daniel, Ezra-Nehemiah, and Chronicles. With this arrangement, in Jesus' day, the Old Testament consisted of twenty-four books.

When Jesus appeared to the disciples just after his resurrection, he alluded to this threefold arrangement of the Scriptures, saying, "'When I was with you before, I told you that everything written about me in the law of Moses and the prophets and in the Psalms must be fulfilled.' Then he opened their minds to understand the Scriptures" (Luke 24:44-45). In this instance, Jesus used the largest book of the Writings, Psalms, to represent that section. Jesus did this with the Latter Prophets when he referred to that section as the writing of "the prophet Isaiah" and then quoted from both its last book, Malachi, and its first book, Isaiah, respectively in Mark 1:2-3.

The Old Testament as we find it today follows the structure and order of the Greek translation of the Old Testament, called the Septuagint (LXX), which divides some of the books thematically. For instance, what might be a single book of Samuel is divided in two—1 Samuel is mostly about King Saul, and 2 Samuel is mostly about King David. It also divided the Twelve into individual books. Additionally, the Septuagint changed the order from the tripartite Hebrew canon. As first compiled, the Old Testament loosely followed a more thematic organization; what we have today, at least from Genesis to Esther, is arranged more chronologically.

Be that as it may, even though the content is the same, today our Old Testament has thirty-nine books with four or five sections according to how one treats the prophetic books. The divisions are the books of law (Genesis, Exodus, Leviticus, Numbers, and Deuteronomy); the books of history (Joshua, Judges, Ruth, 1 & 2 Samuel, 1 & 2 Kings, 1 & 2 Chronicles, Ezra, Nehemiah, and Esther); the books of poetry and wisdom (Job, Psalms, Proverbs, Ecclesiastes, and Song of Songs); and the prophetic books, which may be subdivided into the Major Prophets and the Minor Prophets, a division based on the length of the books (Major Prophets: Isaiah, Jeremiah, Lamentations, Ezekiel, and Daniel; and Minor Prophets: Hosea, Joel, Amos, Obadiah, Jonah, Micah, Nahum, Habakkuk, Zephaniah, Haggai, Zechariah, and Malachi).

So the Old Testament is the collection of thirty-nine books that make up the Law, History, Wisdom, and the Prophets.

Human writers

The Old Testament was written and composed by about forty human authors, mostly in the language of Hebrew and some in Imperial Aramaic, over about a thousand-year period roughly spanning the mid-second to mid-first millennium BC.

Chronologically, it starts with the narrative in Genesis 1 of how God created all things in the beginning. It ends with the book of Nehemiah, which tells how a remnant of God's covenant people had returned to their homeland in Judah after seventy years in Babylonian Exile and finally completed the rebuilding of the wall of Jerusalem in about 445–444 BC.

In summary, the Old Testament is a historical record of God's act of creation and dealing with his creation, with special attention to his relationship with his covenant people, Israel.

The covenants

What is a testament? The word *testament* comes from the Latin *testamentum*, and it means "covenant" or "agreement." Covenants point to the great promises God made in the Scriptures with his people. There is a covenant with Noah, a covenant with Abraham, a covenant with Israel, a covenant with David, and then the new covenant inaugurated by the Lord Jesus Christ. The old covenant refers to the covenant God made with Israel at Mount Sinai. Israel's failure to keep this covenant anticipated the new covenant about which the prophets Jeremiah and Ezekiel prophesied. Through his prophet Jeremiah, God declared,

> "This is the new covenant I will make with the people of Israel after those days," says the LORD. "I will put my instructions deep within them, and I will write them on their hearts. I will be their God, and they will be my people. And they will not need to teach their neighbors, nor will they need to teach their relatives, saying, 'You should know the LORD.' For everyone, from the least to the greatest, will know me already," says the LORD. "And I will forgive their wickedness, and I will never again remember their sins."
>
> JEREMIAH 31:33-34

Speaking of the new covenant through Ezekiel, God said,

> I will give you a new heart, and I will put a new spirit in
> you. I will take out your stony, stubborn heart and give
> you a tender, responsive heart. And I will put my Spirit
> in you so that you will follow my decrees and be careful
> to obey my regulations.
> EZEKIEL 36:26-27

In the upper room at the Lord's Supper, Jesus pronounced his inauguration of the new covenant in Luke 22:20, saying, "This cup is the new covenant between God and his people—an agreement confirmed with my blood, which is poured out as a sacrifice for you."

Consequently, the Old Testament anticipates the New Testament, in particular, the person and work of the Lord Jesus Christ.

Therefore, when considering what the Old Testament is, one should recognize that it is not only the first part of God's magnificent story of redemption but also the largest part of it. From the beginning of Genesis to the end of Revelation, God has revealed his plan of salvation. As God spoke through his prophet Isaiah, he declared, "Only I can tell you the future before it even happens. Everything I plan will come to pass, for I do whatever I wish" (Isaiah 46:10).

Later, we will look more closely at this plan in the discussion concerning understanding the theological context of a passage, but here is a simple overview of the Bible's story of redemption:

1. God created all things.
2. Humanity fell into sin through Adam and Eve in the
   Garden of Eden.

3. God promised that the woman's seed, or descendant, would crush the head of the serpent. From this, the Old Testament anticipates the coming Messiah, who will rule over all the earth and deal with humanity's sin problem. God used Abraham, Israel, David, and others to this end. This section comprises about two-thirds to three-fourths of the Bible's story of redemption.

4. Much of what is anticipated in the Old Testament is fulfilled with the incarnation of Jesus Christ, his birth, sinless life, death, burial, resurrection, and ascension to heaven, where he sits at the right hand of the Father as our advocate and mediator.

5. The church is established and given the mission of spreading the gospel and making disciples.

6. The revelation of a new creation is proclaimed, when God will establish a new heaven and a new earth, and every one of his promises will be fulfilled.

So what is the Old Testament? It is the first thirty-nine books of the Bible, written by about forty human authors, mostly in Hebrew and some in Aramaic. It can be divided into four main sections: the books of the Law, History, Wisdom, and the Prophets. It is a record of the activities of God and his old covenant people, Israel, spanning from Creation to the return of the Jewish exiles from Babylon in the mid-fifth century BC. Also, in anticipating the coming of Jesus, it lays the groundwork for God's revelation of his redemptive plan seen throughout the entirety of Scripture. The Old Testament is the eternal, inerrant, authoritative Word of God, and it is with this focus in mind that we will begin our discussion of why to study the Old Testament.

PART I

CONSIDERATIONS WHEN TEACHING THE OLD TESTAMENT

ONE DAY MY HEBREW PROFESSOR IN seminary entered the classroom obviously agitated. After glaring down at his books, he finally looked up at us and said, "I don't know why I do this, because none of you are going to preach from the Old Testament anyhow."

Before that, as a young pastor I had not thought much about it, but from then on, I began regularly teaching from the Old Testament. As I did, my congregation and I grew in our appreciation for the Hebrew Scriptures. After ten years, I believed God was calling me to return to seminary so I could teach the Old Testament in higher education and encourage others to teach it as well in their ministries. I hoped my students would discover the richness of its treasures and experience the joy of revealing it to others.

When I told my friends I was returning to seminary, they

understood because they knew my love for God's Word. However, when I told them I was planning to study the Old Testament, they looked befuddled.

"Why the Old Testament?"

Some even asked me, "Why not study something *important*, like the New Testament or theology?" I heard these remarks so many times that I vowed to make sure people knew the answer to "Why the Old Testament?" whenever I had the opportunity.

I began to realize just how neglected the Old Testament is in pulpits and Bible studies in many churches today. In twenty-plus years of teaching a survey of the Old Testament, I've found that about half my students have received little to no significant instruction in the Old Testament before coming to seminary. Many of their pastors will preach through books of the Bible, but rarely if ever through an Old Testament book. I've even had students ask me why New Testament believers should bother with studying the Old Testament.

I have come to realize that when I teach the Old Testament to evangelical Christians, there will be many who have little background in it and others who don't believe there is any value to studying it. Students have indicated to me that before coming into an Old Testament survey class, they really wondered if there was anything they could learn that would be beneficial to them as New Testament believers.

In teaching, everything begins with *what* and *why*. They are entwined. The answer to *what* always leads to *why*. The answer to *why* is grounded in the answer to *what*.

The introduction began with answers to the question "What is the Old Testament?" Now we need to answer why it's essential for believers today to study and know it. A deeper understanding of that answer is necessary to know why we should teach it.

1

The Old Testament Is the Word of God

The Old Testament is more than the record of an ancient people, more than just a collection of religious texts, and more than a compilation of wise teachings. It may seem obvious, but when one studies, teaches, or preaches the Old Testament, it's essential to remember that it is the Word of God.

This truth has not always been recognized by everyone throughout the history of the church. For instance, in the mid-second century, Marcion rejected the Old Testament because he believed the malevolent creator "god" (the so-called Demiurge) depicted in the Old Testament, who ordered the slaughter of multitudes of human beings, whose laws were oppressive, and who was generally antagonistic toward people was incompatible with Jesus, the gracious, loving God in the New Testament.

However, this became a problem given that the apostle John

reveals that nothing was created except through Jesus, the Word who was God and became human (John 1:1-4, 14). In fact, most of the New Testament became a problem for Marcion for two reasons: (1) The writings in the New Testament are intricately connected to the Old Testament; and (2) The New Testament authors referred to the Old Testament as the Scriptures, the Word of God.

As a result, Marcion focused on the apostle Paul's writings, especially those that make a distinction between the law in the Old Testament, which to Marcion represented the Old Testament god, and the gospel in the New Testament, which represents the God of compassion and grace. According to Marcion, Jesus came to rescue people from the god of the Old Testament along with his laws and ruthless ways.

To eliminate every reference and allusion to the Old Testament in the New Testament, Marcion's version of the Bible included sections of Paul's writings and a revised version of the Gospel of Luke.

The leaders of the church rejected Marcion's views, understanding that both Testaments are the revelation of the one and only eternal God. They recognized that the God who is the Creator and who revealed himself to Abraham, Moses, and the prophets in the Old Testament is the same God who has revealed himself in the person and work of Jesus in the New Testament. They also affirmed that the Old Testament is the eternal Word of God.[1]

Even so, many of the issues Marcion had with the Old Testament are shared by people in the church today.[2] Therefore, let's consider what the Old Testament authors, the New Testament authors, and Jesus himself said about the Old Testament.

The Old Testament Authors

In the Old Testament, the authors clearly affirm that they are speaking and recording God's Word.

For example, when the Lord gave his law to Israel, he said to Moses, "Give these instructions to the family of Jacob; announce it to the descendants of Israel" (Exodus 19:3); and when the people of Israel were preparing to enter into the Promised Land, Moses said, "These are the commands, decrees, and regulations that the LORD your God commanded me to teach you" (Deuteronomy 6:1).

Also, Deuteronomy 31:24-26 specifies that when Moses finished writing the Book of Instruction he received from God, he commanded the Levites to place it beside the Ark of the Covenant.

Summarizing the laws, Leviticus 26:46 indicates that "These are the decrees, regulations, and instructions that the LORD gave through Moses on Mount Sinai as evidence of the relationship between himself and the Israelites."

Moses was only one of many prophets who recorded the Word of God. When Israel rejected the Lord and turned instead to Egypt, God instructed Isaiah, "Now go and write down these words. Write them in a book. They will stand until the end of time as a witness that these people are stubborn rebels who refuse to pay attention to the LORD's instructions" (Isaiah 30:8-9).

Similarly, Jeremiah 36:1-2 records, "During the fourth year that Jehoiakim son of Josiah was king in Judah, the LORD gave this message to Jeremiah: 'Get a scroll, and write down all my messages against Israel, Judah, and the other nations. Begin with the first message back in the days of Josiah, and write down every message, right up to the present time.'"

When King Jehoiakim burned the scroll, the Lord gave Jeremiah another message. He said, "Get another scroll, and write everything again just as you did on the scroll King Jehoiakim burned. Then say to the king, 'This is what the LORD says . . .'" (Jeremiah 36:28-29).

Speaking of God's prophets, the author of 2 Kings writes,

"Again and again the LORD had sent his prophets and seers to warn both Israel and Judah: 'Turn from all your evil ways. Obey my commands and decrees—the entire law that I commanded your ancestors to obey, and that I gave you through my servants the prophets'" (2 Kings 17:13).

The Old Testament authors speak of several attributes of the Old Testament that demonstrate it is the Word of God. For instance, Isaiah proclaims, "The grass withers and the flowers fade, but the word of our God stands forever" (Isaiah 40:8). Also, through his prophet Isaiah, the Lord proclaims, "Only I can tell you the future before it even happens. Everything I plan will come to pass, for I do whatever I wish" (Isaiah 46:10), and that "my word . . . will accomplish all I want it to, and it will prosper everywhere I send it" (Isaiah 55:11).

The psalmist in Psalm 111:7-8 says that the Lord's "commandments are trustworthy. They are forever true." The psalmist also declares, "Your eternal word, O LORD, stands firm in heaven. . . . Your regulations remain true to this day, for everything serves your plans" (Psalm 119:89, 91). Accordingly, the Old Testament testifies to its being the eternal Word of God and not obsolete. It will accomplish what God wants to accomplish with it in both the present and the future.

In Psalm 19:7-9, after declaring the majesty of God revealed by all of creation, David delineates several characteristics of God's Word and its impact on the people of God, using six synonyms referring to various nuances of God's Word: *perfect, trustworthy, right, clear, pure,* and *true.* Though the Hebrew word *torah* at times refers specifically to the legislative material of the Pentateuch, in this context, as often in the Psalms, it seems to refer more generally to all of the written revelation of God's Word and is therefore translated "the instructions of the LORD" in verse 7.

Let's take a more in-depth look at these attributes of God's Word:

1. God's Word is *perfect*—that is, blameless or without defect. God's perfect Word brings us back from going the wrong way while refreshing, reviving, and restoring our vigor for the abundant life that he intends for us to live (Psalm 19:7).

2. God's Word is *trustworthy*, meaning it has been confirmed to be reliable. The Word of God makes wise those who are inexperienced, naive, and unwittingly headed for trouble (Psalm 19:7).

3. God's Word is altogether *right* and *applicable to all of life*. Therefore, it is a source of extreme joy (Psalm 19:8; see also Jeremiah 15:16).

4. God's Word is *clear*. As a result, it gives *insight* to those who look to it (Psalm 19:8).

5. God's Word is *pure*, and he inspires pure reverence from his people (Psalm 19:9). *Pure* means spotless, without blemish, free from contamination. It is the opposite of defiled, unclean, corrupted, and impure. In Psalm 12:6, David declares that the promises of the Lord "are pure, like silver refined in a furnace, purified seven times over."

Though the biblical authors never use the word *inerrant*, that the Bible is free from any error is irrefutably inferred, given that it is God's *perfect, trustworthy, right, clear,* and *pure* revelation of himself.

Declaring that the Scriptures are *inerrant* is stronger than asserting they are *infallible*. In some circles, *infallible* means that the Bible is without error in matters of faith and theology but not necessarily error-free in all matters. However, as noted above, David's statements in Psalm 12 and 19 under the inspiration of the Holy Spirit clearly establish the inerrancy of Scripture.[3] Furthermore, just as God is from everlasting to everlasting, so is his inerrant Word (Deuteronomy 33:27; Psalm 90:2; 119:89-90; Isaiah 40:28).

Robert Plummer provides a list of matters one must consider to avoid misunderstanding the inerrancy of the Scriptures:

a) "Inerrancy applies only to the autographs (original copies of Scripture)."

b) "Inerrancy respects the authorial intent of the passage and the literary conventions under which the author wrote."

c) "Inerrancy allows for partial reporting, paraphrasing, and summarizing."

d) "Inerrancy allows for phenomenological language (that is, the description of phenomena as they are observed and experienced)."

e) "Inerrancy allows the reporting of speech without the endorsement of the truthfulness of that speech (or the implication that everything else said by that person is truthful)."

f) "Inerrancy does not mean that the Bible provides definitive or exhaustive information on every topic."

g) "Inerrancy is not invalidated by colloquial or nonstandard grammar or spelling."[4]

6. God's Word is *true* (Psalm 19:9). It is firm and dependable. Consequently, one can trust it to be just and to uphold righteousness. Numbers 23:19 states, "God is not a man, so he does not lie. He is not human, so he does not change his mind. Has he ever spoken and failed to act? Has he ever promised and not carried it through?" The Scriptures are God's revelation of himself and consequently a reflection of his character. Thus, we can trust that what we read in the Bible is true.

Clearly the Old Testament authors understood that their writings and the words they contain are the inerrant Word of God, that their writings would continue to achieve God's purposes for which they were given, and therefore that they would never cease to be the Word of God.

The New Testament Authors

Conservatively, there are two hundred or more quotations of the Old Testament in the 7,957 verses in the New Testament. However, some argue that there are about one thousand allusions to Old Testament passages in the New Testament. If this is accurate, then about one of every eight verses in the New Testament refers in some way to the Old Testament. Even so, did the authors of the New Testament demonstrate a conviction that the Old Testament is the Word of God?

The New Testament writers referred to the Old Testament as "Scripture" or "the Scriptures," using the Greek word *graphē*, which literally means "a writing." It reveals they understood that the Old Testament is the Word of God.

Matthew demonstrates this in his Gospel. In Matthew 26:56, he affirms that the writings of the prophets are "recorded in the Scriptures."

Luke does this as well. When Jesus met a couple of his disciples on their way to Emmaus shortly after Jesus' crucifixion, Luke writes, "Then Jesus took them through the writings of Moses and all the prophets, explaining from all the Scriptures the things concerning himself" (Luke 24:27). The two disciples Jesus spoke with referred to the writings of Moses and all the prophets as the Scriptures also (Luke 24:32). Then when Jesus later met with his disciples, Luke equates what Jesus taught about himself "in the law of Moses and the prophets and in the Psalms" as the Scriptures (Luke 24:44-45).

The apostle John picked up on this regarding Jesus' resurrection indicating, "After he was raised from the dead, his disciples remembered he had said this, and they believed both the Scriptures and what Jesus had said" (John 2:22).

James and Peter also refer to the Old Testament as Scripture. Quoting Leviticus 19:18, James writes, "It is good when you obey the royal law as found in the Scriptures: 'Love your neighbor as yourself'" (James 2:8). James most likely calls it "the royal law" because Jesus also quoted this verse as being one of the two most important verses of the entire law in the Old Testament (Matthew 22:36-40). Furthermore, James quotes Genesis 15:6, declaring it as fulfilled Scripture (James 2:23). James 4:6 also quotes Proverbs 3:34: "As the Scriptures say, 'God opposes the proud but gives grace to the humble." And Peter recognizes as Scripture Isaiah's prophecy concerning the Messiah, when he quotes Isaiah 28:16 in 1 Peter 2:6.

What's more, though the book of Hebrews doesn't use the word *Scriptures,* the author's arguments and exhortations are thoroughly entrenched with Old Testament motifs such as the sacrifices and priesthood. Along with the books of James and Revelation, Hebrews sounds much like an Old Testament book in places—including right from the beginning: "Long ago God spoke many times and in many ways to our ancestors through the prophets." (Hebrews 1:1).

The apostle Paul also refers to the Old Testament as Scripture or the Scriptures. For example, in Romans 1:2, he refers to the Prophets as part of "the holy Scriptures." In Romans 4:3, as Paul declares that salvation is by faith and not by works, he quotes Genesis 15:6 as "the Scriptures" declaring, "For the Scriptures tell us, 'Abraham believed God, and God counted him as righteous because of his faith.'"

In Romans 9:17, the apostle references the Pharaoh in Egypt who opposed Moses in Exodus 9:16 and calls this passage "the Scriptures." In Galatians 4:30, speaking of Sarah and Hagar in Genesis 21, Paul calls this passage "the Scriptures." These examples show that Paul understood that the Old Testament is the Word of God.

Paul not only calls the Old Testament the Scriptures or Scripture, but he also reveals that "all Scripture is inspired by God" in 2 Timothy 3:16. The literal translation of the word rendered "inspired" is "God-breathed" or "breathed out by God," indicating that the Scriptures, all of the books of the Old Testament along with the New Testament writings existing at that time, were produced by God's breath and are therefore from God. The words in the Old Testament are God's words.

In 2 Peter 1:20-21, Peter makes a similar declaration concerning Old Testament prophecy, stating that "you must realize that no prophecy in Scripture ever came from the prophet's own understanding, or from human initiative. No, those prophets were moved by the Holy Spirit, and they spoke from God."

When contemplating the meaning of the inspiration of Scripture, it is prudent to clarify the difference between the terms *revelation* and *inspiration*. *Revelation* refers to how God discloses or reveals himself—who he is and what he does. *Inspiration* refers to the truth that the Bible is the Word of God.[5]

This truth that the Old Testament is the Word of God lays the groundwork for understanding that the New Testament books are also Scripture. Peter instructs believers that they should regard the New Testament books with the same authority as the books of the Old Testament. In 2 Peter 3:16, he writes of those who twisted Paul's "letters to mean something quite different, just as they do with other parts of Scripture." As Guy Prentiss Waters correctly states,

> The apostles not only confirm that the Old Testament is the inspired Word of God but instruct the church to regard the books of the New Testament as having precisely the same authority as the books of the Old Testament. The unbroken testimony of the apostles is that the books of both Testaments are in their entirety special revelation, the inspired Word of God.[6]

Given these points, it is clear the New Testament writers understood that the Old Testament is the Word of God and that rather than being a replacement of the Old Testament, the New Testament is an expansion of the Word of God. While believers today may say, "Even the Old Testament is the inspired Word of God," the apostles were saying that, along with the Old Testament, "Even the New Testament is the authoritative Word of God."

The Words of Jesus

The writers of both Testaments recognized that the Old Testament is the Word of God, but what did Jesus say about it? Like the New

Testament authors, he referred to the Old Testament as "Scripture" or "the Scriptures."

For instance, when Satan tempted Jesus in the wilderness, Jesus quoted Deuteronomy 8:3, Deuteronomy 6:16, and Deuteronomy 6:13 as the authoritative Word of God to rebuff the tempter (Matthew 4:1-11). Also, when Jesus cleansed the Temple of the money changers, he quoted Isaiah 56:7 proclaiming, "The Scriptures declare, 'My Temple will be called a house of prayer'" (Matthew 21:13). And when Jesus returned to the Temple and the Jewish leaders questioned his authority, he quoted Psalm 118:22-23, calling these verses "the Scriptures" as he applied this passage to himself and rebuked them (Matthew 21:42; Mark 12:10).

Responding to the Sadducees concerning life after death, Jesus said, "But now, as to whether there will be a resurrection of the dead—haven't you ever read about this in the Scriptures? Long after Abraham, Isaac, and Jacob had died, God said, 'I am the God of Abraham, the God of Isaac, and the God of Jacob.' So he is the God of the living, not the dead" (Matthew 22:31-32). In this instance, Jesus quoted the words God spoke to Moses at the burning bush on Mount Sinai (Exodus 3:6) and called them "the Scriptures."

On another occasion, when Jesus and his disciples had completed their Passover meal and were headed toward the Mount of Olives, he told them they all would desert him. Next, Jesus told them that when they abandoned him it would be in fulfillment of the Scriptures (Matthew 26:30-31, referencing Zechariah 13:7).

Luke records that when Jesus visited his boyhood village of Nazareth, he went to the synagogue and "stood up to read the Scriptures" (Luke 4:16). Then he took the scroll of Isaiah the prophet and read Isaiah 61:1-2. When he finished reading, Jesus said, "The Scripture you've just heard has been fulfilled this very day!" (Luke 4:21).

As Jesus states in Matthew 5:17, "Don't misunderstand why I have come. I did not come to abolish the law of Moses or the writings of the prophets. No, I came to accomplish their purpose."

Certainly, Jesus demonstrated that the Old Testament is the eternal, authoritative Word of God. For instance, when the Pharisees attempted to trap Jesus concerning marriage and divorce in Matthew 19:1-9, he responded by quoting Genesis 1:27, stating that God "made them male and female." Next, he quoted Genesis 2:24, stating that this "'explains why a man leaves his father and mother and is joined to his wife, and the two are united into one.' Since they are no longer two but one, let no one split apart what God has joined together" (Matthew 19:5-6).

Using the Old Testament as an authoritative source, Jesus teaches that God created humankind, from the beginning, as male and female. God also established the institution of marriage, defined as a male and female joining together and becoming one flesh, and that no one should split apart what God has joined together.

In this chapter, we've begun addressing necessary considerations to make in preparation for teaching the Old Testament. The first consideration is that the Old Testament is the Word of God. It is eternal, inerrant, authoritative, and inspired by God. Both the Old Testament and New Testament authors attest to this truth in their writings, and Jesus attests to it also.

When teaching the Old Testament, we must recognize that we're teaching more than just an ancient book filled with historical information, words of wisdom, and moral platitudes from a time and culture far removed from ours. It is much more than that. The Old Testament is the eternally trustworthy Word of God, just as Agur son of Jakeh exclaims in Proverbs 30:5: "Every word of God proves true."

2

The Old Testament Is God's Revelation of Himself

THERE ARE A NUMBER OF WAYS WE CAN TRULY get to know other people. For instance, what they say about themselves, what they have done in the past, and what they communicate about their intentions for the future all help us get to know them.

With this in mind, this section will discuss how the Old Testament is God's revelation of himself—first by looking at some of his attributes, and then by surveying some of his actions that had immediate and future implications.

This discussion will also serve as an outline of the theological context of the Old Testament. Given the nature and length of this work, a sampling of examples from the biblical text will have to suffice to make the point that the Old Testament is God's revelation of himself.

The Old Testament Reveals Who God Is

The various names of God in the Old Testament reveal who he is. Here is a partial list:

Adonai (Lord, Master): Genesis 15:2

Elohim (God): Genesis 1:1

El Elyon (The Most High God): Genesis 14:18

El Olam (The Everlasting God): Genesis 21:33

El Shaddai (God Almighty): Genesis 17:1

El Qanna (The Jealous God): Exodus 20:5

Yahweh (LORD, God's personal covenant name to Israel):
  Genesis 2:4

Yahweh Go'ali (The Lord My Redeemer): Psalm 19:14

Yahweh Yireh (The Lord Will Provide): Genesis 22:14

Yahweh Mekoddishkem (The Lord Who Makes You Holy):
  Exodus 31:13

Yahweh Nissi (The Lord My Banner): Exodus 17:15

Yahweh Rapha (The Lord Who Heals): Exodus 15:26

Yahweh Rohi (The Lord My Shepherd): Psalm 23:1

Yahweh Sabaoth (The Lord of Heaven's Armies):
  1 Samuel 1:3

Yahweh Shalom (The Lord Is Peace): Judges 6:24

Yahweh Shammah (The Lord Is There): Ezekiel 48:35

Yahweh Tsidkenu (The Lord Our Righteousness):
  Jeremiah 23:6

Yahweh Tsuri (The Lord My Rock): Psalm 19:14[1]

Furthermore, in the Pentateuch, God is also called "The Fear of Isaac" (Genesis 31:42, NIV), "The Mighty One of Jacob" (Genesis 49:24), and "Father" (Isaiah 63:16). All the names attributed to God in the Old Testament reveal some aspect of his identity.

What are some other things the Old Testament reveals about who God is?

God wants us to know him.

Genesis 1:1 and every verse of Scripture that follows reveals that God wants to be known by us and that he has revealed himself to us through his Word. More than eighty times in the Old Testament God speaks and acts so that either his covenant people Israel or the nations might know that he is "the LORD."

The fact that we have both the Old and New Testament from the inspiration of the Holy Spirit shows that God wants us to know him. Certainly, the incarnation of Christ demonstrates this also, but before Jesus was born and the New Testament was written, God had already revealed that he is a God who is committed to making himself known through his words and actions as revealed in the Old Testament.

God is the Creator.

The Old Testament reveals that God is the Creator—which means that everything in the universe *begins* with God, *comes* from God, and is *sustained* by God. Moses poetically prayed to the Lord, "Before the mountains were born, before you gave birth to the earth and the world, from beginning to end, you are God" (Psalm 90:2). As the Creator, and not part of creation, God is the one who sustains everything (Psalm 36:6; 145:16-17).

It also means that everything *belongs* to God, and therefore he has full authority over all creation. Moses proclaimed to Israel, "You must always obey the LORD's commands and decrees that I am giving you today for your own good. Look, the highest heavens and the earth and everything in it all belong to the LORD your God" (Deuteronomy 10:13-14). David wrote, "The earth is the

LORD's, and everything in it. The world and all its people belong to him" (Psalm 24:1).

The truth that God is the Creator demonstrates that he has power over all creation. Jeremiah wrote, "The LORD made the earth by his power, and he preserves it by his wisdom. With his own understanding he stretched out the heavens. When he speaks in the thunder, the heavens roar with rain. He causes the clouds to rise over the earth. He sends the lightning with the rain and releases the wind from his storehouses" (Jeremiah 10:12-13).

When the Old Testament reveals that God is the Creator, it says as much about who he is as it says about what he has done. To recognize God is the Creator is to recognize his omnipotence and sovereignty over all creation. It is to proclaim along with the psalmist, "Our God is in the heavens, and he does as he wishes (Psalm 115:3).

God is the only God.

The Old Testament also reveals that God is the only God. This is the doctrine of monotheism. As the Israelites were about to cross over the Jordan River into the land of Canaan, Moses reminded them that God allowed them to witness "trials, miraculous signs, wonders, war, a strong hand, a powerful arm, and terrifying acts" so that they would "know that the LORD is God and there is no other" (Deuteronomy 4:34-35).

Isaiah declares, "This is what the LORD says—Israel's King and Redeemer, the LORD of Heaven's Armies: 'I am the First and the Last; there is no other God. . . . You are my witnesses—is there any other God? No!'" (Isaiah 44:6, 8). Given that it was God's purpose to make himself known to the nations through his people Israel, it was imperative that they devote themselves to the one true God and forsake all of the false gods of the nations (Isaiah 43:8-13).

Isaiah 44:8 speaks of both God's strength and his immutability: "There is no other Rock—not one!" God does not change. He communicated this truth when he revealed himself to Moses as "I AM WHO I AM" in the burning bush at Mount Sinai (Exodus 3:1-2, 14).

Concerning this revelation, T. Desmond Alexander explains that God was revealing to Moses (and through him to Israel, God's covenant people) "the idea that God will be true to his own nature: 'I will be who I am' or 'I am who I will be.' 'God can be counted on to be who God is.'"[2] Likewise, through the prophet Malachi, the Lord succinctly declared to his covenant people, "I am the LORD, and I do not change" (Malachi 3:6).

God is wise.

Given the amount of Wisdom Literature in the Old Testament, it is fitting to recognize that the Old Testament also reveals that God is wise. Isaiah proclaimed that the Lord's counsel is wonderful and that he gives great wisdom (Isaiah 28:29). When God revealed to Daniel the meaning of King Nebuchadnezzar's dream, Daniel praised God and exclaimed that God "has all wisdom and power" and that he is the one who gives wisdom to those who are wise (Daniel 2:20-21).

To say that God is wise means that God is inherently right or righteous, he knows what is right and does what is right in the right way, at the right time, and to the right extent. Job also realized that only God is the source of true wisdom (Job 28:12-28), and Solomon teaches that the Lord is eager to give wisdom to those who seek it (Proverbs 2:1-12).

When one receives wisdom from God, one will rightly devote one's life to live for the Lord in reverence and awe of him. God is wise, God is the source of wisdom, and God is the goal of wisdom.

God is holy.

The last attribute we will consider that God reveals of himself in the Old Testament is that he is holy. God told Moses to instruct the people of Israel, "You must be holy because I, the LORD your God, am holy" (Leviticus 19:2), and in a vision of God on his throne, Isaiah heard this proclamation: "Holy, holy, holy is the LORD of Heaven's Armies! The whole earth is filled with his glory!" (Isaiah 6:3). In this vision, Isaiah realized he needed to be made pure, and his message to Israel revealed the nation's need for it as well (Isaiah 1:18).

The basic root meaning of the main Hebrew word translated "holy" is "cut" or "set apart." It is also closely related to the idea of purity.[3] Consequently, Mark Rooker rightly observes, "Holiness is the sphere of purity unique only to God."[4]

God's holiness applies to all his other attributes. God is at once transcendent, supreme, complete, and altogether pure. He is holy in all things. Hannah communicated this truth well when she prayed, "No one is holy like the LORD! There is no one besides you; there is no Rock like our God" (1 Samuel 2:2).

These are just some of the attributes attested to in the Old Testament to reveal who God is. Entire books have been dedicated to studying the attributes of God shown in the Bible.[5] The examples given show that one way the Old Testament demonstrates that it is God's revelation of himself is by revealing his wondrous attributes.

The Old Testament Reveals What God Has Done

Just as it was impossible to list all of God's attributes revealed in the Old Testament, it is also not possible to discuss everything God did that the Old Testament authors recorded. Still, by looking at seven major events in the Old Testament, we can see God's self-revelation through his actions.

The Creation, the Fall, the Flood, the establishment of a covenant with Abraham, the Exodus and the covenant at Mount Sinai, the establishment of God's covenant with David, and the Exile are all significant events in the Old Testament where God reveals something about himself.

Creation

What do God's actions in the Genesis 1-2 account of Creation reveal about him?

1. God created everything.

2. God speaks. Everything came into being by his word. This is noteworthy, given that John refers to Jesus as "the Word" when he writes, "In the beginning the Word already existed. The Word was with God, and the Word was God. He existed in the beginning with God. God created everything through him, and nothing was created except through him. The Word gave life to everything that was created" (John 1:1-4).

3. God created everything in an orderly fashion. He is a God of order. He made everything to function as he established it to function. For instance, he created male and female. To deny this truth is to rebel against God as the Creator.

4. God created humans in his image. He created us from dust such that we bear a resemblance to other creatures, while at the same time we are spiritual beings who are to reflect God, know him, and enjoy him forever. While God cares

for all of his creation, there is something uniquely special about his affection for human beings (Psalm 8).

5. God made everything good. This truth anticipates the numerous declarations in the Old Testament that God is good (1 Chronicles 16:34; Psalm 25:8; 145:9; Ezra 3:11).

6. Genesis 2:1-3 indicates that when God was finished with his work of creation, he rested. This lays the foundation for the Sabbath in the Old Testament law and ultimately for the rest that believers have in Christ (Exodus 20:8-11; Hebrews 4).

The Fall

In Genesis 3, the Fall refers to the moment when sin entered the human race. What should we learn about God through his actions when Adam and Eve sinned in the Garden of Eden?

1. God warns people of the danger of sin and its consequences. In Genesis 2:16-17, God told Adam that he may eat the fruit of every tree in the Garden except for the fruit from the tree of the knowledge of good and evil, and that if Adam did eat its fruit, he was "sure to die." Going forward in the Old Testament, God repeatedly warns his people of sin and its consequences through his messengers, the prophets.

2. God allowed the serpent into the Garden to tempt Eve. The text provides no explanation as to why God allowed this to happen, but from then on, experiencing temptation to sin against God is common to every person who has the ability to reason right from wrong.

3. God allowed Adam and Eve to sin. Here again, no reason for this is given in the text. However, Romans 9:22-24 indicates that both the Fall along with God's work of redemption display his supreme glory.

4. God graciously sought Adam and Eve after they sinned and attempted to hide themselves from him. He is a God who seeks and saves sinners.

5. God held Adam, Eve, and the serpent accountable for what they had done. One major consequence was that God barred Adam and Eve from having access to the tree of life. Throughout the Scriptures, God holds sinners accountable for their sin.

6. God clothed Adam and Eve with animal skins. This act foreshadows the day when the Lord will clothe in righteousness those who believe in his Son (Philippians 3:9).

The Flood

God reveals several things about himself through his actions in the Flood account of Genesis 6-8.

1. God pays attention to the deeds of the wicked and the righteous.

2. God was grieved by humanity's wickedness but was pleased with Noah's righteousness.

3. God declared that he was going to destroy every living thing on the earth with a flood, with the exception of Noah, his family, and every type of creature on the earth. God judges the wicked but shows favor to the righteous.

4. God provided Noah a way to be saved from the flood by instructing him to build the ark. Thus, the God who pronounces judgment is the God who provides a way to be saved for those who trust and obey him.

5. God did what he said he would do both in his judgment and salvation. God is faithful to keep his word.

6. God promised that he would never again curse the ground or destroy every living thing, even though the human race is bent toward evil from childhood. Not only is God just, but he is also merciful.

The covenant with Abraham

One of the most significant occasions in all the Scriptures is when God made a covenant with Abraham. Keith H. Essex articulates its importance when he claims, "The Abrahamic Covenant undergirds the totality of the biblical revelation."[6] When God made his covenant with Abraham, he laid a foundation for the rest of Scripture in both Testaments going forward. The details of this covenant are found in Genesis 12, 15, and 17. Genesis 12:1-3 is noteworthy because it includes the first recorded words that God spoke to Abraham, and it is here that he initiates his covenant with Abraham.

In the Old Testament, a covenant is the establishment of a bond between two parties both legally and relationally. The agreement to establish a covenant may involve responsibilities required by both parties for the covenant to stand (often called a bilateral covenant); in other cases, the initiation and fulfillment of the covenant expectations may fall primarily on one of the parties (often called a unilateral covenant). What can we observe in Genesis 12:1-3 about the covenant that God made with Abraham?

1. God initiated the covenant with Abraham.

2. God made promises to Abraham. He promised to (a) make Abraham into a great nation, (b) bless him, (c) make him a man of renown, (d) bless those who blessed Abraham, and (e) curse those who mistreated him.

3. God is committed to fulfilling his covenant promises to his people.

4. God's purpose for blessing Abraham was not only for Abraham's sake. God chose Abraham to be his instrument of blessing to people from every nation, which is communicated twice for emphasis in these three verses.

5. God revealed to Abraham that the covenant would be everlasting (Genesis 17:1-8). The Abrahamic covenant was a unilateral covenant because God initiated it and committed himself alone to fulfilling it (Genesis 15:1-20), while at the same time he expected Abraham's obedience within the confines of its terms (Genesis 17:9).

   It is similar to the new covenant in Christ. God initiated it and he alone fulfills it. Believers make no contribution to their salvation—it is by grace through faith and not of "the good things we have done" (Ephesians 2:8-9). Nevertheless, those who are recipients of salvation by grace through faith in Jesus have been created "anew in Christ Jesus, so we can do the good things he planned for us long ago" (Ephesians 2:10).

The Exodus and covenant at Mount Sinai

Because of movies and Sunday school classes, perhaps one of the most well-known events in the Old Testament is the Exodus, recorded in Exodus 12–15, along with what happened soon after with the giving of the Ten Commandments at Mount Sinai in Exodus 19–20. What did God reveal about himself in these momentous events?

1. God heard the cries of his people and was responsive to them (Exodus 14:15-18).

2. God protected his people from their enemies before defeating their enemies (Exodus 14:19-20).

3. God displayed his glory through defeating Pharaoh and his army (Exodus 14:17; 15:6, 11). God is committed to making his glory known to both his people and his enemies.

4. God saved his people and destroyed every single one of their enemies (Exodus 14:27-28).

5. Before initiating his covenant with the nation of Israel at Mount Sinai, God revealed to them that his purpose for choosing them as his "own special treasure from among all the peoples of the earth" was so that they would be his "kingdom of priests" and his "holy nation" (Exodus 19:5-6).

6. God gave Israel the Ten Commandments as the framework for the bilateral covenant he made with Israel at Mount Sinai. Based on the fact that God had delivered them from bondage, the Ten Commandments served as the embodiment of the entire Old Testament law, and God expected Israel to obey all of it (Exodus 19:4-5; 20:1-2).

The covenant with David

In 2 Samuel 7, God made an everlasting covenant with David. This passage reveals both what God has done and what he promises to do with David in the future. God began with pointing out how he was always present with his people and had destroyed all of David's enemies (2 Samuel 7:6-9). Next, God made several promises to David.

1. Reminiscent of his promise to Abraham, God promised David that he would make his name famous (2 Samuel 7:9).

2. God promised that sometime in the future he will provide a homeland for Israel that will be peaceful and secure, giving them rest from all their enemies (2 Samuel 7:10).

3. God will establish a Davidic dynasty with a descendant of David sitting on the throne (2 Samuel 7:11).

4. David's son will build the Temple as David had wished to do (2 Samuel 7:13).

5. David's son will be God's son (2 Samuel 7:14). If he sins, God will discipline him, but God will not cut him off like he did Saul (2 Samuel 7:15).

6. God will establish David's throne for eternity; his "throne will be secure forever" (2 Samuel 7:16).

Consequently, God's covenant with David had profound implications connecting Israel's present situation to both its roots and God's purposes for it in the future.

The Davidic covenant functions in the larger story in a number of significant ways. In the history of the people of Israel, it inaugurates a divinely designed model of kingship for the nation. Furthermore, it implements the kingship of Yahweh among his people at a deeper and higher level. In addition to addressing concerns and problems of the developing nation of Israel, the Davidic covenant carries forward in specific ways the intentions and purposes of God expressed in the Sinai covenant and, even further back, in the covenant with Abraham.[7]

Recognizing that the Davidic covenant should be understood in light of the Abrahamic covenant, Eugene Merrill observes,

There are also important connections and correspondences between the Abrahamic and Davidic covenants. . . . The narrator is writing, among other reasons, to clarify that the Davidic dynasty did not spring out of the conditional Mosaic covenant but rather finds its historical and theological roots in the promises to the patriarchs. Israel, as the servant people of Yahweh, might rise or fall, be blessed or cursed, but the Davidic dynasty would remain intact forever because God had pledged to produce through Abraham a line of kings that would find its historical locus in Israel but would have ramifications extending far beyond Israel. The kings (plural) promised to Abraham (Gen. 17:6, 16) became more specifically identified by Jacob as one (singular) to whom the royal scepter and staff would belong (Gen. 49:10). He, this one from Judah . . ."[8]

The Davidic covenant specifies that the kings God promised would come from Abraham will come from "this one from Judah," David.

The Exile

Finally, the exiles are arguably the most calamitous events in ancient Israel's history. In 722 BC, the Assyrians finished the conquest of the northern kingdom of Israel and carried its ten tribes into exile. However, when referring to the Exile, scholars are usually referring to the Babylonian Exile of Judah. Nebuchadnezzar carried out three deportations of Hebrews into captivity. The first was in 605 BC, the second was in 598–597 BC, and the third was in 587–586 BC when the Babylonians destroyed the Temple and all of Jerusalem.

Here are six observations concerning exile in the Old Testament.

1. When the people renewed their covenant with God just before they entered the Promised Land, God warned the Israelites that they would be banished into captivity for their disobedience to this covenant with him. (Deuteronomy 28:36-37, 41, 49-52, 63-68).

2. God sent his prophets to continue to warn the people to repent lest the Lord banish them from the land into exile. From the time they were preparing to enter the Promised Land in 1407–1406 BC to the time the Assyrians and Babylonians carried the people away into exile, God warned them over and over of this covenant curse if they chose to be unfaithful to him.

3. God promised that he would restore them to their land after a time in exile (Deuteronomy 30:1-5).

4. Several prophets preached this message also. Jeremiah even told the Babylonian exiles that they would be in captivity for seventy years and then God would restore them to their

land (Jeremiah 25:9-13; 29:10). In Ezra 1:1-4, we see the fulfillment of this prophecy. Therefore, exile was not God's last word to Israel.

5. God sent Israel into exile because of their covenant infidelity, as seen through four key issues: (a) idolatry, or unfaithfulness to the Lord (1 Chronicles 9:1; Hosea 2:1-8); (b) taking advantage of the weak and poor instead of caring for them (Amos 2:6-7; Micah 2:9); (c) immorality (Hosea 4:2; Micah 2:1-2); and (d) damaging God's reputation among the nations (Ezekiel 36:19-21). Instead of being a blessing to the nations by rightly representing God as a kingdom of priests, Israel instead brought reproach upon his name.

6. God gathered his people together and brought them back to their land because he is a compassionate God who is faithful to his covenant even when his people are not, and he is zealous for protecting his reputation among the nations (Ezekiel 36:22-38; Micah 7:15-20).

Doubtless, all the events in the Old Testament reveal something about God, but this summary includes some of the more significant. They're not only important within their contexts in the Old Testament, but they'll serve us when teaching the Old Testament with a biblical-theological perspective of the entire Scriptures in mind.

This chapter has demonstrated that believers should study the Old Testament because one way God reveals himself to us is through the writings of the Old Testament as they describe who he is, what he has done, and what he intends to do in the future.

3

The Old Testament
Anticipates Jesus

New Testament believers should study the Old Testament not only because it is the Word of God and is God's revelation of himself but also because it speaks of and anticipates the person and work of the Lord Jesus Christ.

Alec Motyer writes, "The Old Testament is Jesus predicted; the Gospels are Jesus revealed; Acts is Jesus preached; the Epistles, Jesus explained; and the Revelation, Jesus expected. He is the climax as well as the substance and centre of the whole."[1]

Several passages in the Old Testament attest to this truth. It is essential to recognize that, during the time of Christ, his followers didn't always readily understand that certain Old Testament prophecies were about him.

G. K. Beale and D. A. Carson state it well: "The same gospel that is sometimes presented as that which has been prophesied and is now fulfilled is at other times presented as that which has been hidden and is now revealed."[2]

Starting at the beginning, Genesis 1–11 reveals how humanity landed itself in the hopeless predicament of sin and sin's consequences because of its willful rebellion against God. When Adam and Eve ate from the tree of the knowledge of good and evil, they discovered that "the wages of sin is death" (Genesis 2:17; 3:19, 22-24; Romans 6:23).

However, in Genesis 3:15, which is often called the *protoevangelium* or "first good news," there is hope because an offspring of the woman will ultimately defeat the serpent, the one John calls "that old serpent, who is the devil, Satan" in Revelation 20:2. The genealogy at the end of Genesis 11 and God's initiation of his covenant with Abraham in Genesis 12 is the beginning of the rest of the story of how God through Christ will defeat the serpent and save humanity.

A second Adam, a descendant of Abraham and David, will crush the head of the serpent. Therefore, Genesis 1–11 also anticipates the promise of a new creation, and just as John 1:1-4 indicates that God created everything through Jesus, everything in the new creation will come about through Jesus as well (Revelation 21:1-7).

Isaiah prophesied that the Lord would create new heavens, a new earth, and a new Jerusalem (Isaiah 65:17-19; 66:22). John caught a glimpse of this as recorded in Revelation 21.

What's more, humanity's moral collapse in Genesis 1–11 provides the reason why people will need to be made new creations in Christ who bear his likeness (2 Corinthians 5:17; 1 Corinthians 15:45-49).

The motif of fall, judgment, and then a restoration that will exceed what had been previously is prevalent in the Old Testament, especially in the messages of the prophets. Ultimately these prophecies will come to an eschatological climax when they are fulfilled by Jesus as depicted in Revelation 19–21.

Understanding Jesus is the Creator in Genesis 1–2 and what happened to creation in Genesis 3–11 anticipates his work of a new creation, the second part of the story that begins in Genesis 11–12.

Paul seems to indicate this in Galatians 3:8-9: "What's more, the Scriptures looked forward to this time when God would make the Gentiles right in his sight because of their faith. God proclaimed this good news to Abraham long ago when he said, 'All nations will be blessed through you.' So all who put their faith in Christ share the same blessing Abraham received because of his faith."

This work of new creation makes little sense apart from the Old Testament texts that lay the foundation for understanding Jesus and his mission. From the beginning, the Bible establishes the need for a savior.

Jesus recognized his purpose in light of the Old Testament's anticipation of him. In Matthew 5:17-18 Jesus said, "Don't misunderstand why I have come. I did not come to abolish the law of Moses or the writings of the prophets. No, I came to accomplish their purpose. I tell you the truth, until heaven and earth disappear, not even the smallest detail of God's law will disappear until its purpose is achieved."

Jesus gives full expression to the meaning of the law. And when the Jewish leaders accused Jesus of disregarding God's law, Jesus rebuked them saying, "You search the Scriptures because you think they give you eternal life. But the Scriptures point to me! . . . If you really believed Moses, you would believe me, because he wrote about me" (John 5:39, 46).

Duane Garrett observes how Jesus embodies the full expression of God's law:

1. **Jesus becomes the Passover Lamb to bring about deliverance from bondage (1 Corinthians 5:7).** One can also say that, as the Passover Lamb, it is Jesus' shed blood that saves one from God's judgment (Romans 5:9).

2. **Jesus is the realization of the requirements of the law and is the man who embodies the ideal image of God (Matthew 5:17).** Jesus expressed his love for his heavenly Father through faithful obedience and loved others to the point of laying down his life for them (John 14:31; Romans 5:8).

3. **Jesus is the one and only perfect sacrifice that makes atonement for sin (Hebrews 2:17), he removes all impurity (Hebrews 9:13-14), and he cleared the way so that one may have access to God (Matthew 27:51).** Consequently, we can observe that Jesus suffered and died to make his people holy as he is holy by means of his own blood (Hebrews 13:12).

4. **Jesus is the true tent of meeting who pitched his tent among his people and sojourns with them (John 1:14).**[3]

What's more, Jesus identified himself using Old Testament expressions. For example, Jesus often referred to himself as "the Son of Man." This expression comes from Daniel 7:13-14 where the Messiah is called "someone like a son of man" to whom "the Ancient One" will give "authority, honor, and sovereignty over all the nations of the world, so that people of every race and nation and language would obey him. His rule is eternal—it will never end. His kingdom will never be destroyed."

In Mark 14:61-64, at one of Jesus' trials, Jesus not only identified himself as the Son of Man, but he also called himself "I AM," the name the Lord used to identify himself to Moses at the burning bush on Mount Sinai (Exodus 3:14). Thus, in this instance, using Old Testament language Jesus identified himself as both the Messiah and as God. The high priest and the other religious leaders certainly understood what Jesus meant, and for this reason they declared that he was guilty of blasphemy and deserved to die.

Besides some distinctive uses of "Son of Man" as Jesus' identity in the Gospel of John, Christopher J. H. Wright recognizes that the ways Jesus employs it fall into three basic categories. The first is in reference to his earthly ministry and his authority over sin, sickness, nature, and the law. The second category refers to his suffering, death, and resurrection. And the third and largest category is in reference to his eschatological role as king and judge.

Wright observes, "Taken together, these three categories are remarkably comprehensive as a way of encapsulating how Jesus saw his own identity as well as how he envisaged his immediate and more long-term destiny."[4]

Andrew G. M. Hamilton comments how interesting it is that Jesus never used the word *Messiah* to refer to himself. However, after he read from the scroll of Isaiah and pronounced that this messianic prophecy was fulfilled that day, Jesus was stating that he is the Messiah. Also, he certainly affirmed that he is the Messiah to the Samaritan woman at Jacob's well in John 4:25-26 and to his enemies in Mark 14:61-62. And when Peter declared to Jesus, "'You are the Messiah, the Son of the Living God.' Jesus replied, 'You are blessed, Simon son of John, because my Father in heaven has revealed this to you'" (Matthew 16:16-17).[5] It is possible that Jesus refrained from using this title himself because there were so many mistaken beliefs and expectations concerning the Messiah in his day.[6]

Numerous citations in the New Testament refer to Old Testament passages that anticipate the coming of Jesus Christ and his mission. The following is a list of thirty of these Old Testament passages and some New Testament verses that cite or allude to them:

The seed of the woman (Genesis 3:15): Romans 16:20; Galatians 4:4; Hebrews 2:14; Revelation 12:9, 17

The Abrahamic covenant (Genesis 12:1-3): Acts 3:24-26; Galatians 3:7-16

A king from Judah (Genesis 49:10): Matthew 2:6, 11; Hebrews 7:14; Revelation 5:5

Passover lamb (Exodus 12:1-51): John 1:29, 36; 19:33, 36; 1 Corinthians 5:7-8; 1 Peter 1:19

Star from Jacob (Numbers 24:17): Revelation 22:16

A prophet like Moses (Deuteronomy 18:15-19): Matthew 13:57; 21:46; Luke 24:19; John 1:21, 25; 6:14; 7:40; Acts 3:22; 7:37

The Davidic covenant (2 Samuel 7:12-16): Matthew 1:1; Luke 1:32-33; Acts 15:15-16

Opposition (Psalm 2:1-2): Acts 4:25-26

Son of God (Psalm 2:7-8): Mark 1:11; Luke 3:22; Acts 13:33; Hebrews 1:5; 5:5

Resurrection (Psalm 16:8-11): Acts 13:35-37

Suffering (Psalm 22): Matthew 27:35, 39, 43-46; Mark 15:34; John 19:23-24

His sovereign rule (Psalm 110:1-4): Matthew 22:41-45; Mark 12:35-37; Luke 20:41-44; Acts 2:34-36; 1 Corinthians 15:25-28; Hebrews 1:3, 13; 4:14–5:10

Judgment (Psalm 110:6): Revelation 19:11-21

Rejected (Psalm 118:22-24): Mark 12:10-11; Acts 4:9-12;
Ephesians 2:20; 1 Peter 2:6-8

Virginal conception (Isaiah 7:14): Matthew 1:22-23;
Luke 1:31-35

A great light (Isaiah 9:1-2): Matthew 4:13-16; Luke 1:76-79;
2:32; John 1:4-5; 8:12; 9:5; 12:46

Deity (Isaiah 9:6-7): Luke 1:32-33; Acts 10:36

A light for the nations (Isaiah 42:1-7): Matthew 12:15-21;
Luke 2:27-32; John 8:12; Revelation 21:23-24

Suffering servant (Isaiah 52:13–53:12): Matthew 8:16-17;
20:28; 26:28; Mark 10:45; 14:24; Luke 9:22; 22:20;
Acts 8:32-35; Hebrews 9:28; 1 Peter 2:21-25

Spirit of the Lord (Isaiah 61:1-2): Luke 4:16-21

Bethlehem atrocity (Jeremiah 31:15): Matthew 2:16-18

A new covenant (Jeremiah 31:31): Matthew 26:28;
Luke 22:20; 2 Corinthians 3:6; Hebrews 8:6-13;
9:15; 12:24

Son of Man (Daniel 7:13-14): Matthew 8:20; 9:6, 10:23;
12:8; 13:41; 16:13, 27; 26:64; Mark 2:10-11; 8:31;
14:62; Luke 5:24; 6:22; 9:22; John 1:51; 3:13-14;
8:28; Acts 7:56; Revelation 1:13; 14:14

Out of Egypt (Hosea 11:1): Matthew 2:13-15

Born in Bethlehem (Micah 5:2): Matthew 2:1-6;
John 7:40-43

Riding on a donkey (Zechariah 9:9): Matthew 21:1-7

Betrayed for thirty pieces of silver (Zechariah 11:12-13):
Matthew 26:14-15; 27:3, 9-10

Pierced (Zechariah 12:10): John 19:31-37; Revelation 1:7

Preceded by a messenger (Malachi 3:1): Matthew 11:10;
Mark 1:2; Luke 1:76

Preceded by Elijah (Malachi 4:5-6): Matthew 11:14-15; 16:14; 17:9-13; Mark 6:14-16; 9:11-13; Luke 1:16-17; John 1:21

The preceding list is by no means comprehensive, but it demonstrates how the New Testament writers and Jesus himself recognized that the Old Testament speaks of and anticipates the coming of the Savior.

4

The Old Testament Lays the Foundation for the New Testament

In light of the fact that the Old Testament speaks of and anticipates Jesus, it is no surprise that the authors of the New Testament used the Old Testament extensively as the foundation for their writings. It's beyond the scope of this work to demonstrate this fact comprehensively, but the task has been done well by others.[1]

We'll begin with the introductions of the Gospels as examples of how those writers showed that the Old Testament is foundational as they introduce the Lord Jesus Christ. Then, we will highlight a few ways in which the other New Testament authors did so as well.

Matthew

Matthew's Gospel arguably contains fifty-five quotations or partial quotations of Old Testament passages. Possibly the reason

Matthew is placed first in the New Testament canon is because of its clear and frequent links to the Old Testament.[2] In the first verse of his book, Matthew introduces Jesus as "the Messiah." *Messiah* is a transliteration of the Hebrew word *mashiach*, which appears thirty-nine times in the Old Testament. It means "anointed" or "anointed one." In the New Testament, the equivalent Greek word *christos* ("Christ," also meaning "anointed one") is used.

R. T. France states that in conjunction with Old Testament prophecies, "It seems clear that the title 'Messiah' would, for most ordinary Jews, have pointed to a coming king of the line of David, whom God would send to restore his people to national independence and to their rightful pre-eminence as the people of God."[3]

What's more, the Old Testament anticipates that the Messiah will rule over *all* the nations and establish justice, peace, and blessing on earth. Matthew then introduces the record of Jesus the Messiah's ancestors by stating that Jesus is "a descendant of David and of Abraham" (Matthew 1:1). In effect, by right away calling Jesus "the Messiah" and "a descendant of David," Matthew begins presenting evidence that Jesus is the fulfillment of the Davidic covenant.

Furthermore, by indicating Jesus is a descendant of Abraham, Matthew connects Jesus to the Abrahamic covenant. In Genesis 12:1-3, God reveals to Abraham (Abram) that God has chosen him and his descendants for the purpose of being a blessing to the nations.

God's wording of this is even more explicit in Genesis 18:18-19: "For Abraham will certainly become a great and mighty nation, and all the nations of the earth will be blessed through him. I have singled him out so that he will direct his sons and their families to keep the way of the LORD by doing what is right and just. Then I will do for Abraham all that I have promised" (see also Genesis 22:18).

The Lord restated this promise both to Isaac and his son Jacob, whose name was changed to Israel (Genesis 26:4; 28:14).

The point is that when Matthew begins his Gospel, he demonstrates that Jesus is the Messiah by connecting him to the Abrahamic covenant and its fulfillment through the genealogical line of Abraham, which leads to Jesus.

In Matthew 1:1, the apostle lays the foundation for the rest of his Gospel. France summarizes the theological emphasis of Matthew in this way:

> The essential key to all Matthew's theology is that in
> Jesus all God's purposes have come to fulfilment. . . .
> Everything is related to Jesus. The Old Testament points
> forward to him; its law is 'fulfilled' in his teaching; he is
> the true Israel through whom God's plans for his people
> now go forward; the future no less than the present is
> to be understood as the working out of the ministry of
> Jesus. History revolves around him, in that his coming is
> the turning-point at which the age of preparation gives
> way to the age of fulfilment. Matthew leaves no room for
> any idea of the fulfilment of God's purposes, whether for
> Israel or in any other respect, which is not focused in this
> theme of *fulfilment in Jesus*.[4]

We will only fully understand the revelation of who Jesus is if we begin at the beginning of his story in the Old Testament and follow it to its fulfillment and climax in the New Testament. Matthew conveys this message by his introduction and the genealogy that follows which contains the names of individuals who are pertinent to his story.

Mark

There are at least sixty-nine Old Testament references in the Gospel of Mark.[5] Like Matthew, when Mark begins his Gospel, he first calls Jesus "the Messiah, the Son of God" (Mark 1:1). This expression also connects Jesus to the Davidic covenant and emphasizes that the Messiah will be God's Son (2 Samuel 7:14).

Next, Mark quotes the Old Testament prophets' predictions of the messenger God would send to prepare the way for the Messiah. This messenger is John the Baptist (Mark 1:2-4; Malachi 3:1; Isaiah 40:3).

Mark's description of Jesus' baptism (Mark 1:9-11) echoes the Servant Song of Isaiah 42 where the Lord says of his servant, "Look at my servant, whom I strengthen. He is my chosen one, who pleases me. I have put my Spirit upon him" (Isaiah 42:1). Thus, Mark uses the Old Testament in his introduction, showing that an understanding of Jesus' fulfillment of the Old Testament promises is foundational for understanding who Jesus is.

Luke

Luke appears to quote the Old Testament about thirty times, but one could argue that he *alludes* to the Old Testament hundreds of times. Pao and Schnabel concur that "Luke's references to the law of Moses, the prophets, and the psalms clearly express his conviction that the person and ministry of Jesus, as well as the Christian communities and their message, are based on the Jewish Scriptures."[6]

In Luke 1, the apostle introduces his book recalling the prophecies concerning the coming of a prophet like Elijah who will prepare the way for the Messiah (Luke 1:13-17; Isaiah 40:3; Malachi 3:1; 4:5-6). Then Luke turns his attention to Gabriel's announcement that Mary will conceive by the Holy Spirit and give birth to

Jesus. And like Matthew and Mark, the language in this passage echoes aspects of the Davidic covenant: "He will be very great and will be called the Son of the Most High. The Lord God will give him the throne of his ancestor David. And he will reign over Israel forever; his Kingdom will never end!" (Luke 1:32-33).

Additionally, Zechariah the priest "was filled with the Holy Spirit and gave this prophecy: 'Praise the Lord, the God of Israel . . . He has sent us a mighty Savior from the royal line of his servant David, just as he promised through his holy prophets long ago. Now we will be saved from our enemies and from all who hate us. He has been merciful to our ancestors by remembering his sacred covenant—the covenant he swore with an oath to our ancestor Abraham'" (Luke 1:67-73). This prophecy declares that Jesus is the fulfillment of both the Davidic and Abrahamic covenants.

John

John is also concerned about demonstrating that Jesus fulfilled all the messianic prophecies in the Scriptures concerning him (e.g., John 12:38; 13:18; 19:24, 28, 36-37), and John quotes the Old Testament fourteen times.[7]

However, when he begins his prologue in verses 1-18, he does so a little differently than the other three Gospel writers. In John's case, he immediately demonstrates a connection to the Old Testament with the first three words, "In the beginning," echoing Genesis 1:1. Jesus' beginning did not occur in a manger. In fact, Jesus had no beginning because he already existed before the beginning, as he was with God and is God. What's more, "God created everything through him" (John 1:1-3). What's also amazing is that he became flesh and, reminiscent of God's manifest presence with Israel in the wilderness at the Tabernacle, he "tabernacled" or "pitched a tent" among us on earth (Exodus 25:8-9; 40:34-35).

As he concludes his prologue, John indicates that just as the law was given through Moses by grace, so by grace God's "unfailing love and faithfulness came through Jesus Christ" (John 1:17). Greater than the law of Moses, Jesus is the fulfillment and full expression of it. John not only shows that the law anticipates the coming of the Messiah, but in this verse, he calls Jesus the Christ, which is to say, "the Messiah." This expression, along with calling Jesus "the Father's one and only Son" in John 1:14, recognizes Jesus as the fulfillment of the Davidic covenant.

So all four of the Gospel writers point out early in their writings that in fulfillment of the Davidic covenant, Jesus is the Messiah. Robert D. Bergen observes,

> The significance of the eternal covenant between the Lord and David for the New Testament writers cannot be overemphasized. These words played an essential preparatory role in developing the messianic expectations that were fulfilled in Jesus. The hopes that were raised by the Lord's words—that God would place a seed of David on an eternal throne and establish a kingdom that would never perish—were ones that no Israelite or Judahite monarch satisfied, or even could have satisfied. But they were ones that the first-century Christians understood Jesus to fulfill.[8]

Bergen continues, pointing out seven teachings about Jesus in the New Testament that spring from the Davidic covenant. Jesus is . . .

(1) the son of David (cf. Matthew 1:1; Acts 13:22-23; Romans 1:3; 2 Timothy 2:8; Revelation 22:16, etc.);

(2) one who would rise from the dead (cf. Acts 2:30; 13:23);

(3) the builder of the house for God (cf. John 2:19-22;
  Hebrews 3:3-4, etc.);

(4) the possessor of a throne (cf. Hebrews 1:8; Revelation 3:21,
  etc.);

(5) the possessor of an eternal kingdom (cf. 1 Corinthians
  15:24-25; Ephesians 5:5; Hebrews 1:8; 2 Peter 1:11, etc.);

(6) the son of God (cf. Mark 1:1; John 20:31; Acts 9:20;
  Hebrews 4:14; Revelation 2:18, etc.); and

(7) the product of an immaculate conception, since he had
  God as his Father (cf. Luke 1:32-35).[9]

We can see by these Scripture references that the Gospel writers were not the only ones making connections to the Davidic covenant. Next, we will look at a few examples of how other New Testament writers also used the Old Testament.

Acts

Although the book of Acts is not considered one of the Gospels, it is Luke's second volume, a record of the beginnings of the early church. According to G. J. Steyn and Richard Longenecker, there are at least thirty-six citations from the Old Testament in the book of Acts.[10] Beyond these, there are also many allusions, motifs, and uses of Old Testament language in the book.[11]

The account of Jesus' ascension and the promise of the disciples' baptism with the Holy Spirit (Acts 1:4-11) is reminiscent of 2 Kings 2:9-12 in which Elijah was lifted into heaven by a whirlwind as Elisha watched in anticipation of receiving a double portion of Elijah's spirit.

Shortly after the Ascension, when the disciples were preparing to replace Judas, Peter said, "The Scriptures had to be fulfilled concerning Judas, who guided those who arrested Jesus. This was predicted long ago by the Holy Spirit, speaking through King David" (Acts 1:16). Then, in Acts 1:20, Peter quoted Psalm 69:25 as an imprecatory prayer concerning Judas, followed by a partial quotation of Psalm 109:8 as support for the decision to get a replacement for Judas.

So in the introductory chapter of Luke's account in Acts, he presents the foundational role the Old Testament served from the very beginning of the early church.

Hebrews

Some New Testament scholars debate who wrote the book of Hebrews, but whoever the writer was, the Old Testament is foundational for the book's message.

Speaking of the book of Hebrews, George H. Guthrie states, "No NT book, with perhaps the exception of Revelation, presents a discourse so permeated, so crafted, both at the macro- and microlevels, by various uses to which the older covenant [Old Testament] texts are put, and his appropriation of the text is radically different from the book's apocalyptic cousin."

Guthrie counts "roughly thirty-seven quotations, forty allusions, nineteen cases where OT material is summarized, and thirteen where an OT name or topic is referred to without reference to a specific context," along with numerous echoes throughout the book of Hebrews of the Old Testament.[12] Though pulling mostly from the Psalms, the author of Hebrews also utilizes the Law, the Prophets, and the Writings to communicate his message.

James

In his commentary on the book of James, Douglas J. Moo observes that "The Old Testament also figures prominently in James. To be sure, he does not often formally quote the Old Testament (only in 2:8 [Lev. 19:18]; 2:23 [Gen. 15:6]; and 4:5 [a summary of

OT teaching]). But his language is thoroughly permeated with Old Testament ways of speaking, and he regularly appeals to Old Testament people and stories."[13]

Regarding Old Testament language, in the first verse of his letter, James uses an Old Testament expression, "the twelve tribes" (e.g., Genesis 49:28), to address his Jewish audience. As far as Old Testament people and stories are concerned, in James 2:21, James uses Abraham's willingness to offer his son Isaac on the altar as an illustration of how faith is demonstrated by one's actions, and in James 2:25 he uses Rahab's actions at Jericho to make the same point. In James 5:10-11, James points to the Old Testament prophets and Job as examples to be followed when suffering. And in James 5:16-18, he uses Elijah as an example to remind his audience of the necessity of prayer.

Additionally, in James 2:11, he appeals to the Ten Commandments to encourage his audience to obey God's Word. In places, James' writing also sounds a lot like the book of Proverbs, especially in chapter 3 where he provides instruction concerning how godly behavior practically works out in a believer's life with the humility that comes from the wisdom of God. The language and concerns of the Old Testament so permeate the book of James that Merrill Unger concludes, "If the several passages referring to Christ were eliminated, the whole epistle would be as proper in the canon of the Old Testament as it is in the New Testament."[14]

1 and 2 Peter

In his letters, Peter demonstrates that the Old Testament lays the groundwork for his message. In 1 Peter, about 20 of its 105 verses are Old Testament quotations drawn from books in the Law, the Prophets, and the Writings. First Peter is so saturated with the Old Testament that D. A. Carson observes, "If one were to extend beyond allusions (however defined) to echoes picking up OT language and themes, scarcely a verse in this epistle would be exempt."[15]

Though there are no direct Old Testament quotations in 2 Peter, Peter makes several allusions to Old Testament passages throughout the letter. For example, in 2 Peter 3:13, he refers to the "new heavens and new earth" (see Isaiah 65:17 and Isaiah 66:22). Further, Peter says that, because of what he and the disciples saw of Jesus Christ, "we have even greater confidence in the message proclaimed by the prophets" and "that no prophecy in Scripture ever came from the prophet's own understanding, or from human initiative. No, those prophets were moved by the Holy Spirit, and they spoke from God" (2 Peter 1:19-21).

Paul's letters

The apostle Paul wrote thirteen letters of the New Testament, and he often used the Old Testament to ground his message. Romans, Paul's most theologically dense letter, has about sixty quotations of Old Testament verses.[16] His theological points are chock-full of allusions to the Old Testament.

> As Paul makes clear from the opening of the letter, his message to the church at Rome is nothing more than a proclamation of the Scriptures [i.e., the Old Testament] that have been fulfilled in the incarnate, crucified, and risen Christ. . . . The "gospel of God, concerning his son" is the fulfillment of prophetic promise, and thereby of the message of the whole of Scripture (1:2; 16:25-27). . . . The Scriptures are no mere record of the past. They speak to the present, as do their human authors (4:3, 6; 9:15, 17, 26; 10:6, 8, 11, 16, 20-21; 11:2, 4, 11; 15:12)."[17]

In 1 Corinthians, Paul quotes or partially quotes Old Testament Scriptures at least fifteen times and in 2 Corinthians at least eleven times.[18] It is interesting how he uses the Old Testament law forbidding the muzzling of an ox when it is treading out the grain to instruct the Corinthians that they should provide for his physical needs and the needs of others ministering to them (1 Corinthians 9:9).

Even though there are not explicit quotations of the Old Testament until chapter 3 of Galatians, Paul's dependence on the Old Testament in the letter should be readily apparent. In the first two chapters, Paul's message makes no sense outside of the "conceptual world of the" Old Testament.[19] And Galatians 3–6 include at least ten direct citations of the Old Testament along with several allusions.[20]

In the six chapters of Ephesians there are at least ten full or partial quotations taken from books in the Law, the Prophets, and the Writings, accompanied by more Old Testament allusions.[21] The books of Philippians, Colossians, 1 & 2 Thessalonians, 1 & 2 Timothy, and Titus altogether only contain at most about fifteen partial or full Old Testament citations, and some of these might be better understood as allusions.[22] Nevertheless, Paul's concerns and language in these letters still exhibit the influence of the Old Testament.

Hopefully, this short survey of the New Testament use of the Old Testament has been sufficient to demonstrate that the Old Testament is foundational to the New Testament. The New Testament authors used their Bible, the Old Testament Scriptures, to communicate God's Word to New Testament believers. The more we know and understand the Old Testament, the more we can truly understand the writings of the New Testament.

The Old Testament Gives Wisdom unto Salvation

Most believers speak as if the Good News or the gospel originates in the New Testament. However, if he were with us today, the apostle Paul would beg to differ. Recalling Genesis 15:6, Paul writes, "What's more, the Scriptures looked forward to this time when God would make the Gentiles right in his sight because of their faith. God proclaimed this good news to Abraham long ago when he said, 'All nations will be blessed through you.' So all who put their faith in Christ share the same blessing Abraham received because of his faith" (Galatians 3:8-9). God proclaimed the gospel, the Good News of salvation to Abraham, Abraham believed, and God counted him as righteous because of his faith.

When Paul and Silas were on their missionary journey and entered Berea, they went to the Jewish synagogue there and proclaimed that Jesus is the Messiah. The people "listened eagerly to

Paul's message. They searched the Scriptures day after day to see if Paul and Silas were teaching the truth. As a result, many Jews believed, as did many of the prominent Greek women and men" (Acts 17:11-12). After meticulous and careful examination of the Scriptures (the Old Testament), these people recognized how the Scriptures corroborated what Paul and Silas were declaring concerning the Lord Jesus Christ and came to saving faith in him. This scene demonstrates how God uses the Old Testament to give wisdom unto salvation.

In his second letter to his protégé, Timothy, Paul writes, "But you must remain faithful to the things you have been taught. You know they are true, for you know you can trust those who taught you. You have been taught the holy Scriptures from childhood, and they have given you the wisdom to receive the salvation that comes by trusting in Christ Jesus" (2 Timothy 3:14-15). This is the only time the expression "holy Scriptures" appears in the New Testament, but Josephus used this identical expression when he referred to the Old Testament.[1]

Certainly, Timothy had been taught about the birth, life, death, burial, resurrection, and ascension of Jesus as he came to saving faith in Christ. But given Timothy was taught "the holy Scriptures," it follows that he understood Jesus is the fulfillment of both the Abrahamic and Davidic covenants, that he is the Passover Lamb, that his once and for all sacrifice fulfilled the sacrificial system, that Jesus fulfilled the demands of the law, that he is the prophet greater than Moses, and that he is the promised Servant of the Lord who would restore the tribes of Jacob and be a light for the nations.

Timothy's reception of the Old Testament Scriptures coupled with what he had been taught about Jesus gave him "the wisdom to receive the salvation that comes by trusting in Christ Jesus."

The holy Scriptures communicate God's intention to save sinners through the person and work of the Messiah. The Scriptures alone could not save him, but they enlightened Timothy to recognize and put his faith in the only one who could.[2]

In Acts 2:14-21, when Peter preached on the day of Pentecost, contrary to what one might think, he did not use "The Romans Road" tract to proclaim the gospel. Instead, he began his sermon by quoting Joel 2:28-32. Moses communicated to the Lord his desire that the Lord would pour out his Spirit on all the people of God (Numbers 11:29). Later, Joel prophesied that the Lord would do this as a sign of the last days. Peter quoted Joel to indicate that what his audience was witnessing—the believers speaking in various Gentile languages—was evidence that Joel's prophecy was being fulfilled in front of them. The "glorious day of the LORD" had arrived; the dawn of the messianic age and the day of salvation for "everyone who calls on the name of the LORD" had come (Acts 2:20-21).

Next, Peter declared that the Scriptures attest to the truth that Jesus is the promised Messiah. After rehearsing how Jesus ministered among them, how they responded to him by executing him on the cross, and how God raised him up from the dead, Peter quoted Psalm 16:8-11 to prove that Jesus is the resurrected Messiah, the descendant of David, who conquered death just as David had prophesied and as his followers witnessed.

Then Peter quoted Psalm 110:1 to prove that Jesus alone ascended into heaven to sit at God's right hand and that consequently, Jesus whom they crucified is "both Lord and Messiah" (Acts 2:34-36). When they heard Peter's message, three thousand people believed and were baptized.

Just as the Old Testament gave wisdom unto salvation in ancient Israel, so it does today. My colleague George Martin is a seminary professor and missionary who for many years has traveled to diverse places both domestically and internationally to proclaim the gospel and train others to do so as well. George and those he has trained often share the gospel by beginning in Genesis, introducing God the Creator, and going forward through the Old Testament stories that ultimately lead to the gospel accounts of the life, death, burial, resurrection, and ascension of Jesus.

Dr. Martin has seen unbelievers listen to the stories of the Old Testament, recognize their need for a savior, and come to saving faith in Christ when they discovered that Jesus is both Lord and Savior. Some missionaries in Southeast Asia told him they had never seen a Buddhist come to faith in Jesus without first recognizing that God is the Creator.

There is one God, one Bible, one Savior, and one faith. The Scriptures in their entirety testify to this truth. Therefore, it should be no surprise that the Old Testament gives wisdom unto salvation in the Lord Jesus Christ.

6

The Old Testament Provides Instruction for New Testament Believers

ONE ISSUE THAT CAN BE DETRIMENTAL TO believers today is failure to recognize that the Old Testament is relevant and provides essential instruction for us. Not only did the Law, the Prophets, and the Writings serve the needs of God's people in ancient Israel, but they continue to address the needs of the church today.

As Isaiah stated, "The grass withers and the flowers fade, but the word of our God stands forever" (Isaiah 40:8). The following passages from the New Testament attest to the relevancy of the Old Testament for New Testament believers.

In Romans 15:1-4, Paul instructs believers to follow Christ's example by prioritizing helping others as much as attending to their own needs. Then in Romans 15:3 he calls attention to Christ who "didn't live to please himself." To drive this point home, Paul cites Psalm 69. Here, David describes a time when he was abandoned by his friends, assaulted by his enemies, and humiliated for God's sake. Paul quotes the second part of Psalm 69:9, where David exclaims to the Lord that "the insults of those who insult you have fallen on me." Using this statement in regard to Christ, Paul demonstrates that Jesus desired to glorify his heavenly Father so much that he was willing to forgo pleasing himself and instead endure ridicule aimed at his Father.

With that said, in Romans 15:4 Paul makes a general, parenthetical statement about the Old Testament that anticipates more of his use of it: "Such things were written in the Scriptures long ago to teach us. And the Scriptures give us hope and encouragement as we wait patiently for God's promises to be fulfilled."

Thomas Schreiner observes the significance of Paul's statement:

The OT Scriptures were written "for our instruction,"
that is, for both Jews and Gentiles. By citing the OT
Paul anticipates the scriptural catena in 15:9-12. The
experiences of Christ, reflected in the OT, are a pattern
and model for the church. As the prototype he should be
imitated. The authority of the OT is clearly evident in
this statement (see 2 Tim. 3:16). Paul never understood
the newness of his gospel to nullify the OT. The gospel
fulfilled the Scriptures of old (Rom. 1:2; 3:21, 31; 16:26).
The Scriptures play a vital role in the lives of believers. Not
only are they the source of "instruction" (cf. 2 Tim. 3:16),
but also believers derive "consolation" from them. . . . The
word "consolation" [or encouragement] here means that
believers receive strength and comfort from the Scriptures
to continue living in a way that honors God (cf. 1 Macc.
12:9). In other words, something is wrong if one only

studies the Scriptures academically and does not regularly receive nourishment and strength to live the Christian life. The purpose of the Scriptures is that believers should have "hope." Once again, the immensely practical role of the OT in the lives of Christians is unfolded. Hope is generated through carefully reading, understanding, and obeying the OT.[1]

This truth is highlighted by Paul in his first letter to the Corinthians. As previously mentioned, in 1 Corinthians 9:9, Paul quotes from the Mosaic law in Deuteronomy 25:4, which provided that the ox was to be able to eat from the grain while threshing it. Given that Paul applies this law to people and not animals, it possibly served metaphorically to apply to people in the first place. In the Talmud, the rabbis recognized that this principle applied to laborers as well as to oxen.[2] Paul asks and answers, "Wasn't he actually speaking to us? Yes, *it was written for us*, so that the one who plows and the one who threshes the grain might both expect a share of the harvest" (1 Corinthians 9:10, emphasis added). The main idea in the text is that the principle dictating that oxen should receive provision for their work also applies to those who labor for the sake of the church.

What is fascinating is that Paul, while surely recognizing that this passage was originally given to God's covenant people, Israel, emphatically communicates that New Testament believers need to understand that it was written for their instruction also. Paul continues in 1 Corinthians 10:6 and 11, explaining that the severe consequences the Israelites suffered as a result of their sinful cravings, immorality, and grumbling against God in the wilderness should serve as a warning to New Testament believers. He states that "these things happened *as a warning to us*" and "*as examples for us*. They were written down *to warn us* who live at the end of the age" (emphasis added).

Perhaps the weightiest passage communicating that the Old Testament provides instruction to New Testament believers is 2 Timothy 3:16-17. It begins by stating that "all Scripture is inspired by God and is useful." In Paul's use of the word *graphē* ("Scripture") here, it's possible he was including New Testament writings that had already been written. But given his use of this word in his other writings, how the other authors of the New Testament use it, and how this word is used in relation to the Lord Jesus' teaching, it's safe to assume that Paul is at the very least referring to the Old Testament writings here.

Based on the truth that all Scripture is inspired by God, it follows that all Scripture is also useful and profitable, yielding a practical benefit. How so?

1. It is useful for teaching, for matters of doctrine and conduct.
2. It is useful for rebuking the errors of false teaching and reproving errant behavior.
3. It is useful for correcting or restoring back to living in Christ.
4. It is useful for training believers in righteousness, for equipping them to reflect the character of Christ.

Each of these four beneficial uses of the Scriptures is to be reflected in our preaching, according to 2 Timothy 4:2.[3]

Let's look at an example passage to emphasize that "all Scripture is inspired by God and is useful to teach us what is true and to make us realize what is wrong in our lives," that "it corrects us when we are wrong and teaches us to do what is right," and that "God uses it to prepare and equip his people to do every good work" (2 Timothy 3:16-17).

Nehemiah 3 is a difficult passage for preaching commentaries and Bible studies to address. Many commentaries on the book of Nehemiah skip chapter 3, and I haven't seen any small group Bible study literature that dedicates a session to it. Why is this? It's because the chapter is basically a list of names and people groups who worked on rebuilding the wall of Jerusalem under Nehemiah's oversight. The people were from obscure places with foreign names that are difficult to pronounce. The text lists their locations on the wall, counterclockwise according to proximity to one of the nine city gates. It even lists a gate that many scholars don't agree on regarding its location or function.

How is this material useful and relevant for believers today? We can make several observations from Nehemiah 3 about principles worth knowing and putting into practice. When Nehemiah exhorted the people to do the work that needed to be done . . .

- they responded quickly—they got to work right away;
- they responded voluntarily—no one was coerced to do the Lord's work;
- they responded sacrificially—some left their homes and jobs to do the work;
- they responded in anonymity—many of them are not mentioned by name;
- they responded as a majority—this was not a few doing the work as sometimes is the case;
- they responded cooperatively—they got along with each other as they worked;

- they responded simultaneously—everyone was working at the same time;
- they responded comprehensively—every part of the wall had someone working on it;
- they responded resolutely—they did not quit until the job was done.

Their response was also . . .

- marked by diversity—they came from all walks of life;
- marked by solidarity—they were all working for the same purpose;
- marked by responsibility—each was accountable for a certain section of the wall;
- marked by proximity—they worked side by side;
- marked by practicality—they accomplished the project in a planned, orderly way.

They finished their massive project in just fifty-two days (Nehemiah 6:15). Even this difficult passage contains much to learn regarding how we should think about and do the work to which God has called us. Instead of ignoring this passage, we should profit from the example of these godly people as they responded to God's call.[4]

In this chapter we have looked at how the Old Testament provides instruction for New Testament believers. Paul, especially, demonstrates how all Scripture, the entirety of the Old and New Testaments, is useful for us. Even an ancient law forbidding the muzzling of an ox as it treads out the grain was "written for us" (1 Corinthians 9:10) and is both profitable and relevant for the church today.

With this in mind, Philip Towner observes,

> Paul was not concerned to distinguish between
> the authority of the Old Testament canon and the
> proclamation of the gospel by Jesus and himself, for
> the latter message was the authoritative continuation
> of God's revelation of grace. It brought to clarity what
> the prophets of Israel taught—"anyone who trusts in
> him will never be put to shame" (Rom 10:11, quoting
> Is 28:16) and "everyone who calls on the name of the
> Lord will be saved" (Rom 10:13, quoting Joel 2:32)—
> by announcing that the lordship and resurrection of
> Jesus Christ from the dead form the focal point of our
> faith and our cry to God for salvation (Rom 10:9).
> Ultimately, the Scriptures are relevant and supremely
> useful because they are in their entirety *God's* Word.[5]

Concerning the Old Testament Scriptures, as New Testament believers we need to join Asaph as he exclaims to the Lord in Psalm 73:24, "You guide me with your counsel, leading me to a glorious destiny."

PART II

PREPARING TO TEACH THE OLD TESTAMENT

HAVING GIVEN OUR ATTENTION TO what the Old Testament is and why it's essential to the church, let's now focus on understanding its meaning as we prepare to teach it. Our preparation involves at least three activities: *petition*, *selection*, and *investigation*.

Petition

In the New Testament, the Greek word *deēsis* is a plea for help, a petition to God imploring him to lend his assistance and support. When Paul uses this word in Philippians 4:6, it is translated as "tell God what you need."

Apart from God's aid, it's impossible for us to truly understand his Word, much less teach it to others. We need him to open our hearts and minds to its meaning and implications, to give us the right words and appropriate spirit to communicate his Word, and to know how to rightly apply it to our lives as we encourage others to do the same.

Therefore, the entire preparation process must be immersed in prayer, recognizing our dependency on God to carry out this task. Jesus told his disciples, "Apart from me you can do nothing" (John 15:5).

Acknowledging total dependence on God, we begin by praying.

1. As we desire to be clean vessels used by God (2 Timothy 2:21), we should ask God to reveal sin in our lives and then confess, repent, and ask him "to forgive us our sins and to cleanse us from all wickedness" (1 John 1:9).

2. We must ask God to fill us with his Spirit and make us teachable, to illumine our minds and help us to first receive and apply his Word as we prepare to teach it (John 14:26).

3. We must ask the Lord to help us accurately handle his Word of Truth and protect us from sin (2 Timothy 2:15).

4. We should ask the Father to use his Holy Spirit to help us see how the passage we are studying fits into God's grand narrative and anticipates the person and work of Jesus Christ (John 15:26-27). As we investigate the text, we need to be like David, who prayed, "Open my eyes to see the wonderful truths in your instructions" (Psalm 119:18).

Selection

As we pray, it's time to select a passage. How do we do this? It's best to choose a literary unit, often called a *pericope* in seminary circles. This term comes from the combination of two Greek words that literally mean "cutting around" and gives the idea of a section or portion taken from something larger, like a piece of cake. So a pericope is a literary unit or section of the Scriptures.

Walter Kaiser states, "The pericope is the full story in each episode in the narrative, or the whole poem, to which each of the paragraphs, scenes, or strophes contributes."[1] Usually, a pericope is at least one full paragraph, given a paragraph normally provides the full message of what the biblical author is communicating. In some instances, the pericope might be an entire chapter.

In the Hebrew Bible, we can see how passages are broken into sections, not just as chapters but sometimes as subsections within a chapter. It's useful to know that chapter and verse divisions in our English translations don't always match those in the Hebrew text.

For instance, English translations have seventeen verses in Jonah 1, but the Hebrew text has only sixteen. Jonah 1:17 in English translations is Jonah 2:1 in the Hebrew text. According to the Hebrew text, the first three verses in Jonah form the first pericope with an introduction to God's call to Jonah. The second is 1:4-16, when Jonah runs from God, and the third begins with 1:17 in our English translation and ends with 2:10. Thus, the third pericope in Jonah begins with God's appointment of "a great fish to swallow Jonah."

Therefore, I often choose Jonah 1:1-3 or 1:1-16 for one lesson or sermon and then Jonah 1:17–2:10 for the next. Sometimes I combine the first two pericopes because the first is so small.

Most English translations use headings and subheadings to mark the pericopes for the reader. (The New Living Translation not only does this, but it also shows spacing between paragraphs, which is quite helpful.) If you lack knowledge of Hebrew, a good commentary will inform you of what translators have done with the passage.[2]

Investigation

Once we've selected our biblical text, it's time to begin our investigation of it. A careful examination of the text requires reading thoroughly and purposefully to discover and understand its message.

When beginning an investigation of just about any sort, give attention to answering the following questions: Who? When? Where? How? What? Why? and So what? We need to have these questions continually on our radar as we seek to interpret and comprehend the meaning and purpose of a passage.

It's practical to approach a biblical passage expecting some overlap of these questions. Consequently, as we focus on answering one of these questions, we must keep all of them in mind throughout the process. There is no set order for them. I will address them in the general order I do when preparing to teach, but this order is most comfortable to me and certainly not sacrosanct.

On the other hand, for practical reasons it's best to have a set way to go about this process. If your approach to studying the text is all over the place, most likely your teaching will be all over the place as well, incoherent and incomprehensible. Arguably, this is what characterizes most "bad" teaching.

There is another concern we must beware of when asking these investigative questions. We must keep in mind the principle that Alistair Begg is known for advancing: "The main things are the plain things and the plain things are the main things."[3] In other words, beware of getting bogged down in the mire of excessive, extraneous details that are difficult to understand or that have little or nothing to do with the actual message of the passage.

For instance, in the book of Exodus, Moses had several encounters with the pharaoh of Egypt, but the Bible never mentions the name of this pharaoh. Scholars have written pages in articles and books discussing which king of Egypt he was. It's very interesting and can inform us concerning Old Testament chronology, but when it comes to the message of the text, it really does not matter who he was. Who the pharaoh was is not the point, or as Begg might say, it is neither the "plain" thing nor the "main" thing.

Ultimately, we must always keep in mind the purpose of our investigation: to discover the plain meaning of the text. This begins with seeking to understand what the author's words meant in his original context to his original audience. The correct meaning of a passage is grounded in the author's intent. We should never begin with, "What does this mean to me?" Instead, we must begin with, "What did this mean to the one who wrote it?" If Moses were to hear our teaching of Deuteronomy 4:1-8, our hope is that he would exclaim, "That's exactly what I meant to say!"

Let me use a simple illustration to make this point. Let's say my wife says to me, "Tomorrow morning the trash collectors are coming to pick up our trash. So you need to take out the trash and put it on the curb before then." The next morning, she looks in her closet and discovers all her clothes are missing and asks me if I know what happened.

My response is "You told me to take out the trash, so I did." At this point, it becomes clear that what she meant by *trash* and what I thought *trash* should mean are two very different things. Moreover, my imposing my meaning on what she meant would surely have dangerous and tragic results for me.

The illustration above is silly, but there is nothing trivial about failing to understand the author's intent in God's Word and misrepresenting what it means, whether we do so purposefully or even accidentally. When it comes to interpreting God's Word, what matters first and foremost is what the original author meant.

We also must do the work of *exegesis*—examining the text to "pull out" the meaning—and not *eisegesis*, "reading into" the text something that is not actually there. It usually involves inserting a preconceived idea into a passage that contradicts the intention of its author and that would not have been obvious to its original audience. This almost always happens when one allegorizes the text, like when someone espouses that Rahab's scarlet thread should be understood as the blood of Christ, that the wood Isaac carried up Mount Moriah is a reference to the cross, or that breasts in the Song of Songs represent the Old and New Testaments from which we get the milk of God's Word. This approach makes the Bible mean whatever one thinks it *should* mean and demonstrates a low view of the Scriptures, communicating that the plain meaning of a passage is inadequate.

Some will argue that allegorizing is a sound approach as long as the interpretation can be corroborated somewhere in the Bible. However, this is flawed logic because in order for this to work, one must take the plain meaning of a passage somewhere else in the Bible. Picking and choosing when to allegorize and when to use the plain meaning contradicts the basic principles of communication. With this approach, the intended meaning of the biblical author under the Holy Spirit's inspiration in the original context is no longer primary. Instead, the interpreter becomes the authority over the text according to what best suits his or her own purposes.

Proper interpretation calls for proper exegesis—the process of lifting the meaning of the text from the actual meaning of the words in their original context. It emphasizes the determination to understand the author's intent. Accordingly, *exposition* is drawing out what the text means along with its implications and applications. Teachers of the Word must avoid eisegesis and focus instead on exegesis and exposition to uphold the integrity of the text and faithfully communicate its meaning.

Howard G. Hendricks and William D. Hendricks understand exegesis to be a process of "re-creation": "We're attempting to stand in the author's shoes and recreate his experience—to think as he thought, to feel as he felt, and to decide as he decided. We're asking, What did this mean to him? before we ever ask, What does this mean to us?"[4]

While this statement appears to communicate a spirit of focusing on authorial intent, it also provides us with a warning: Beware of assuming we can know what the biblical authors were thinking or feeling unless they tell us. We must not presume to know their mental, emotional, and psychological states as they wrote. It is impossible to "think as he thought, to feel as he felt, and to decide as he decided" unless he reveals these things to us. Why? Because these are in the private realm, while what they wrote is in the public realm.[5] The meaning and purpose of a passage is in the words the author wrote, not in what his opinion was—unless he reveals it under the inspiration of the Holy Spirit.

As we examine the text, we are to be detectives like Sherlock Holmes, thoroughly investigating and recreating a crime scene to understand everything possible about what was said and done leading up to the crime and everything that happened when it was committed. Of course, we must ask, "What does this mean for the church today and for me personally?" However, these questions cannot be accurately answered until we begin where the text itself began.

Finally, a host of Bible study resources can help in this process. Bible dictionaries and concordances provide answers to questions about words or subjects. Bible atlases are indispensable when trying to understand historical geography.

Commentaries also offer a treasure trove of aids. If possible, it's good to use a technical commentary, an expositional commentary, and then a devotional commentary. Though admittedly, using too many commentaries can get cumbersome. If only using one, then expositional commentaries are usually best because most contain some accessible explanations of issues without getting too technical and also contain some devotional comments without overly spiritualizing the text.[6] Using these resources should complement your own investigation and not become a substitute for it.

7

Who?

WHEN WE ASK THE QUESTION *WHO* WE ARE seeking to discover every person or people group mentioned or even immediately implied in the passage. This begins with "Who was the author?"

Of course, given all Scripture is inspired by God or God-breathed, we must always be mindful that God is the ultimate author of his Word. Next, we should attempt to discover who the human author is that God used to write the passage. In many instances, especially in the Old Testament, the text does not reveal the human author (e.g., 1 and 2 Chronicles).

On the other hand, Jeremiah 36:4 tells us that Jeremiah dictated his messages to his associate, Baruch, who wrote them on a scroll. When the Scriptures don't reveal who the human author is, it isn't pertinent to the meaning of the text. But when they do, as in Jeremiah's case, it is essential information. Knowing about

Jeremiah's authorship of the scroll is necessary for understanding King Zedekiah's failed attempt to snuff out God's Word by burning and destroying the scroll section by section (Jeremiah 36:21-25).

Next, it's important to ask who is delivering the message. It may be the author, like Jeremiah. Or in other instances, the author may not be the one delivering God's message in the narrative, like the time Elijah pronounced in 1 Kings 17:1 that God was about to cause a three-year drought in Israel.

It is just as important to ask who initially received the message. For example, Elijah was addressing King Ahab of Israel when he declared God was sending the drought. As we delve more into the Bible, we realize that Elijah was God's prophet and King Ahab was wicked, leading his people to worship Baal, the storm god, who was believed by his devotees to be the one who supplied Israel's agricultural society with precious rain. What's more, as the vast majority of the people of Israel followed their king, this message was not only meant for the king but also for every Israelite.

With this in mind, we should recognize that every book in the Old Testament canon was first written for God's covenant people, Israel, as its original recipients and audience. As another example, when Moses wrote the Pentateuch, the original recipients were the people of Israel in Moses' day—not anyone before or after that time.

In our investigation of the text, we must begin with who wrote it, who delivered the message, and who first received the message, along with any other people mentioned in the passage. Then we need to learn as much as we can about each of them. Answering some of our other investigative questions will help us with this.

8

When?

ASKING THE QUESTION *WHEN* IS SIMPLY ASKING, "When was this text written?" and "When did the events happen?" The first question addresses the literary context, and the second addresses the historical-cultural context. Seeking to find out when the text was written is connected to the previous questions of "Who wrote it?" and "Who was the original audience to receive it?"

As already noted, it is difficult to know who the human authors are for many Old Testament books, and this leads to speculation about when those books were written. Some biblical commentaries inform us of the issues involved with these two questions. It's usually easier to determine when the events took place than when the book was written.

But even this is not always the case. Many of the psalms of David describe what appear to be events in his life, but some of them don't provide enough information to know exactly when they occurred. Again, when the text does not provide these details, it means they are not essential to getting the message of the passage. The general nature of David's description of his sufferings and feelings of alienation, for instance, consoles the readers in their sufferings, which may be caused by something different than what caused David's sufferings. Nevertheless, the sufferings and emotions of the reader may be every bit as difficult as those of David.

Regardless of the particular historical contextual details that may be absent in some of these psalms, they exhort readers to trust God and seek him as their refuge. One might argue that the lack of historical details in these psalms broadens their reach to all who at one time or another experience suffering and feelings of alienation from God. Sometimes the text provides little to no information about the historical-cultural context, but when it does, it can be very helpful in gaining deeper insight into the meaning of a passage.

Gordon Fee and Douglas Stuart provide an excellent explanation, stating the historical-cultural context, "which will differ from book to book, has to do with several things: the time and culture of the author and his readers, that is, the geographical, topographical, and political factors that are relevant to the author's setting; and the occasion of the book, letter, psalm, prophetic oracle, or other genre."[1] This context basically includes everything concerning what is written in a passage that does not involve the actual words in the passage.[2]

But how is knowing this information pertinent to understanding the meaning of an Old Testament passage? Why give attention to these matters? Scott Duvall and Daniel Hays provide an excellent answer:

Why bother to become familiar with the original historical-cultural context? We do so because it offers us a window into what God was saying to the biblical audience. Since we live in a very different context, we must recapture God's original intended meaning as reflected in the text and framed by the ancient historical-cultural context. Once we understand the meaning of the text in its original context, we can apply it to our lives in ways that will be just as relevant. God's Word is eternally relevant. Our task as students of his Word is to discover that relevance by doing our contextual homework.[3]

Let's look at some examples.

- Knowing about the ancient practice of making covenants provides insight to the numerous covenants recorded in the Old Testament and their significance for the entirety of the Scriptures.
- We can better understand the messages of the prophets when we are familiar with the beliefs and gods of ancient Canaanite religion, especially when the text indicates that the prophets confronted those who worshiped Baal and Asherah.
- Beginning in Deuteronomy, a lot of material in the Old Testament is about exile. Many Old Testament texts make sense only when read in light of God's exiling his covenant people from the Promised Land and his message of restoration, which includes their return to the land.

Because language is an expression of culture, giving attention to the biblical languages will help us understand ancient Israelite culture and aid our understanding of the text's meaning by noting how the people communicated with one another. Thus, for example, extra-biblical inscriptions written in ancient Semitic dialects not only provide chronological clues, but they also help us comprehend what happened and how people communicated those events.

Due to a lack of historical data, and because of different presuppositions and interpretive approaches to both history and the Bible, biblical historians are not all in agreement about when some events in the Bible took place. That said, here is a general time line for the historical periods in the Old Testament and the biblical texts that speak to these events:

1. Before the Flood or the Primeval Period (from Creation until the Flood; Genesis 1–7)
2. After the Flood (after the Flood until the call of Abraham; Genesis 8–11)
3. The Patriarchal Period (ca. 2000 BC to 1806 BC from the call of Abraham until the death of Joseph; Genesis 12–50)
4. Bondage in Egypt and the Exodus (ca. 1806 BC to 1447–1446 BC from the death of Joseph until the crossing of the Red Sea; Exodus 1–14)[4]
5. The Wilderness (ca. 1447–1446 BC to 1407–1406 BC from the crossing of the Red Sea to the crossing of the Jordan River into the land of Canaan; Exodus 15–40, Leviticus, Numbers, Deuteronomy, and Joshua 1–3)
6. The Conquest (1407–1406 BC to 1360–1350 BC from entrance into the Promise Land until the beginning of Israel's judges; Joshua 4–24)

7. The Judges (1360–1350 BC to 1051 BC from Joshua's death until the anointing of King Saul; Judges, Ruth, and 1 Samuel 1–9)

8. The United Monarchy (1051 BC to 931 BC from the anointing of King Saul until the death of King Solomon; 1 Samuel 10–31; 2 Samuel; 1 Kings 1–11; 1 Chronicles 10–29; and 2 Chronicles 1–9)

9. The Divided Monarchies (931 BC to 722 BC from division of the northern kingdom of Israel from the southern kingdom of Judah until the Assyrian exile of the northern kingdom; 1 Kings 12–22; 2 Kings 1–17; and 2 Chronicles 10–28)

10. Judah Alone (722 BC to 587–586 BC from the Assyrian exile of the northern kingdom until the destruction of Jerusalem and the Temple; 2 Kings 18–24; and 2 Chronicles 29–36)

11. The Babylonian Exile (605 BC to 537–536 BC from the first deportation of Jews into exile until the first return of Jews back to Jerusalem led by Zerubbabel; 2 Kings 25, sections of Jeremiah, Ezekiel, Daniel, and Ezra 1–2)

12. The Return from Babylonian Exile (537–536 BC to 445–444 BC from the first return of Jews from Babylonian Exile until the third return from exile led by Nehemiah; Ezra, Nehemiah, and Esther)

Every passage in the Old Testament should be understood within the context of these major periods and events in Old Testament history.[5] We can expect some slight variances in the specific dates. The following chart provides a time line of the kings and prophets of ancient Israel.[6]

Chronology of the Hebrew Kingdoms

THE UNITED MONARCHY

Saul   ca. 1051 BC – ca. 1011 BC
David   ca. 1011 BC – ca. 971 BC
Solomon ca. 971 BC – ca. 931 BC

Temple construction begins ca. 967 BC

THE DIVIDED KINGDOM

Judah: King Rehoboam 931 BC – 913 BC
    Israel: King Jeroboam I 931 BC – 910 BC
Judah: King Abijam 913 BC – 911 BC
    Israel: King Nadab I 910 BC – 909 BC
Judah: King Asa 911 BC – 870 BC
    Israel: King Baasha 909 BC – 886 BC
    Israel: King Elah 886 BC – 885 BC
    Israel: King Zimri 885 BC
    Israel: King Omri 885 BC – 874 BC
Judah: King Jehoshaphat 872 BC – 848 BC
    Israel: King Ahab 874 BC – 853 BC
    Israel: King Ahaziah 853 BC – 852 BC
Judah: King Jehoram 848 BC – 841 BC
    Israel: King Jehoram 852 BC – 841 BC
Judah: King Ahaziah 841 BC
    Israel: King Jehu 841 BC – 814 BC
Judah: King Athaliah 841 BC – 835 BC
Judah: King Joash 835 BC – 796 BC
Prophet in Judah: Joel 810 BC – 795 BC
    Israel: King Jehoahaz 814 BC – 798 BC
Judah: King Amaziah 796 BC – 767 BC
Prophet in Judah: Jonah ca. 800 BC
    Israel: King Jehoash 798 BC – 782 BC
Judah: King Azariah/Uzziah 792 BC – 740 BC
Prophet in Judah: Isaiah 740 BC – 680 BC
    Israel: King Jeroboam II 793 BC – 753 BC

Prophet in Israel: Amos 760 BC – 746 BC
    Israel: King Zechariah 753 BC – 752 BC
    Israel: King Shallum 752 BC
Judah: King Jotham 750 BC – 732 BC
Prophet in Judah: Micah 735 BC – 690 BC
    Israel: King Menahem 752 BC – 742 BC
Prophet in Israel: Hosea 753 BC – 724 BC
Judah: King Ahaz 735 BC – 716 BC
    Israel: King Pekahiah 742 BC – 740 BC
    Israel: King Pekah 740 BC – 732 BC
Judah: King Hezekiah 716 BC – 687 BC
    Israel: King Hoshea 732 BC – 723 BC

FALL OF SAMARIA (ca. 722 BC)

Judah: King Manasseh 697 BC – 643 BC
    Prophet in Judah: Nahum 663 BC – 612 BC
Judah: King Amon 643 BC – 641 BC
    Prophet in Judah: Zephaniah 640 BC – 630 BC
Judah: King Josiah 641 BC – 609 BC
    Prophet in Judah: Jeremiah 626 BC – 585 BC
Judah: King Jehoahaz 609 BC
    Prophet in Judah: Habakkuk 608 BC – 597 BC
Judah: King Jehoiakim 609 BC – 597 BC
    Prophet in Judah: Obadiah after 586 BC
Judah: King Jehoiachin 597 BC
    Prophet in Judah: Daniel 600 BC – 530 BC
Judah: King Zedekiah 597 BC – 586 BC
    Prophet in Judah: Ezekiel 592 BC – 570 BC

FALL OF JERUSALEM (ca. 587 BC)

Second Temple built 520 BC – 516 BC
    Prophet in Judah: Zechariah 519 BC – 475 BC
Ezra's return 457 BC
Nehemiah's return 445 BC
    Prophet in Judah: Malachi ca. 435 BC

9

Where?

As we investigate an Old Testament text, we should be mindful of where the events happened.

Howard F. Vos writes that, along with studying the history and archaeology of the Scriptures, a study of the "geography of the Bible lands sheds light upon the biblical text, giving understanding to it. Also, it helps, to give a sense of reality to the life and times of the Bible. By this means the people and the events of the Bible may emerge from a dusty past to assume current factuality."[1] Therefore it is essential we answer the question *where*.

The question of *where* deals with the author's geographical location when he wrote the text or where the events occurred. Certainly, this question is closely connected to *when,* but it is worth receiving attention on its own.

Why is answering the question *where* important to understanding the meaning of a passage? Here are three key reasons:

1. The message of the Bible is linked to the land. As Paul H. Wright observes, "The land of ancient Israel was entrusted to Abraham, grazed by Jacob, anticipated by Moses, settled by Joshua, ruled by David, tilled by Naboth, evoked by the psalmists, embraced by Isaiah, wept over by Jeremiah, left but not forsaken by Daniel and restored by Ezra and Nehemiah."[2]

   Though the geographical details pertinent to the author's message are sometimes assumed, the text often includes those details so the reader can better understand the message. Sometimes the geographical details are the focus. To comprehend the text, it is important to try to determine where the author was and where the events happened.

2. Geographical details in the Scriptures corroborate that the events in the Bible actually happened to real people in real times at real places. In the realm of apologetics, these details are a counter to those who would trivialize the Bible as a collection of fictional, religious stories.

3. The land in the Bible has biblical-theological significance. For example, as part of his covenant with Abraham, God promised him that he would give his descendants a specific land with specific borders, later called the land of Canaan by the biblical authors (Genesis 12:1; 15:7-21). In the Old Testament, the Promised Land is God's inheritance to his covenant people. It all belongs to him, while at the same time he has given this inheritance to them.

   Moses wrote Deuteronomy in Moab, just across the Jordan River from Canaan. Deuteronomy contains Moses' last words of exhortation and warning to the Israelites before they entered the Promised Land. This is significant in light of how Israel's failure to heed the warning resulted in only a partial conquest of Canaan, and later, during the period of the judges, a time when "all the people did whatever seemed right in their own eyes" (Judges 21:25). Moreover, Israel's future expulsion from that land resulted from their refusal to listen to Moses' instructions and warnings in Deuteronomy 28.

Also, the geographical information at the beginning of the book of Amos provides insight into the dynamics of his ministry. Amos was from Tekoa in Judah during the time of the divided monarchies of Israel in the north and Judah in the south. These two kingdoms had a recent history of conflict between them, and the northerners had an air of superiority, looking down upon the people of Judah. God sent Amos, a man from a disrespected people, to preach an unwelcome message to an unreceptive audience in the northern kingdom. In this instance, answering *where* is as much a geopolitical issue as it is a geographical concern.

Another example is Jeremiah's prophecy in Jeremiah 4:5-19, where he foretold that God was "bringing terrible destruction upon [Judah] from the north" (verse 6). Jeremiah was speaking of the Babylonians. However, Babylon was located directly east of Judah, on the opposite side of the Syro-Arabian Desert. So why did Jeremiah say they would be coming from the north? Because of the Syro-Arabian Desert. There was not enough water in the desert to provide for armies traveling from Mesopotamia to ancient Israel. Therefore, they traveled north along the waters of the Euphrates River and then turned west, then south, to bypass the desert. So the Babylonian invasion of Judah came from the north.

Jeremiah said that Judah's destruction would be announced from Dan, the northernmost city of Israel, and from Ephraim, just north of Judah, as the Babylonians drew closer to wreak destruction (verse 15). Failing to consider the geographical details mentioned in this passage ignores the reality of Jeremiah's message and diminishes the ominous nature of it.

Ezekiel provides another example of the importance of geography to the biblical text. While Jeremiah was preaching in Judah, Ezekiel was taken into Babylonian captivity along with Judah's King Jehoiachin when Nebuchadnezzar's second deportation of Jews occurred in 597 BC (Ezekiel 1:1-3; 2 Kings 24:12, 15-16). Their captivity was in fulfillment of several warnings God issued to his covenant people through his prophets beginning with Moses (e.g., Deuteronomy 28).

In exile, Ezekiel confronted his fellow exiled Jews with their refusal to take responsibility for the sins that led to their captivity. What's more, while in Babylon, Ezekiel not only foretold the cataclysmic destruction of Jerusalem and the Temple but also of God's future plans to restore both Zion and David's throne. The restoration of Jerusalem began with the three returns to Jerusalem led by Zerubbabel, Ezra, and Nehemiah respectively.

In the New Testament, we come to realize that this restoration is ultimately fulfilled in Jesus Christ. Even though Ezekiel and the people of God were hundreds of miles away from home in what appeared to be a hopeless situation in captivity, God had not abandoned them. His prophet delivered messages foretelling of more difficulty in their near future, but that was not God's final word. The Lord who had caused them to be taken into exile would also return them home and one day restore Jerusalem and the Temple to a glory greater than it had ever seen. The location where Ezekiel prophesied was closely connected to the contents of his messages.

These examples will have to suffice, but hopefully they demonstrate the importance of answering the question *where* when seeking to understand the message, meaning, and even the relevance of a passage in the Bible, especially one in the Old Testament. As we carry out the task of investigating an Old Testament text, we always should be mindful of the geographical information included, along with the passage's geographical context. As we conclude this chapter, note Paul H. Wright's insight concerning this matter:

> The Bible's preoccupation with place prompts us as readers to pay attention to the grounded contexts where the events recorded on its pages occurred. In our rush for relevance, we would do well not to forget the points of geographical reference that the text already had for its original readers. When the Bible's authors made the effort to include the specific geographical information in their work, with items as minute as single place names, they intended these bits of data to be an important part of what they had to say. As a result, knowing something of the landed context of the Bible is a necessary prelude for recognizing, interpreting, and applying the other, more "practical" aspects of the biblical text to our lives.[3]

10

How?

Whoever first said or wrote the words "Context is everything" demonstrated great insight because it is nearly impossible to understand the meaning of anything apart from its context.

We have discussed the importance of answering *when* by addressing the historical-cultural context of a passage, and the question of *where* by addressing its geographical context. Yet there is another necessary context one must examine when seeking to understand the meaning of a passage. Let me introduce its significance with an example.

Consider the statement "Mary had a little lamb." What does this statement mean? It could mean Mary was a little girl who had a pet lamb. One can go online and see several illustrations depicting this statement with a little girl enjoying the company of her little pet lamb.

Or a shepherd in a pasture might point to his flock, where a lamb is following its mother. The shepherd might say, "Over there is my ewe Mary, who just gave birth to that little lamb."

Or perhaps Mary and her husband were celebrating their wedding anniversary by going to a nice restaurant with Mediterranean cuisine. Mary was on a diet, and because lamb is generally low in calories, "Mary had a little lamb" with her salad. Here are three examples where one could say the same words but communicate three very different ideas.

In this example, context is everything. Of course, the lyrics to the children's song "Mary Had a Little Lamb" indicate that the illustrations online have it right—the little lamb was Mary's pet. How do we know this? Because the rest of the words in the song provide more information to indicate how the statement should be understood; they provide literary context.

Similarly, when we investigate a passage of Scripture and ask the question *how*, we are seeking to understand the story's surrounding and literary contexts. The surrounding context consists of the passages before and after the focal passage, and the literary context consists of determining what form the author chose to write the text.

The Surrounding Context

The surrounding context of an Old Testament passage should be approached systematically, beginning with the immediate context of the verses before and after the focal passage, then with the rest of the book in which it's located, next with other writings by the same author, then within the remainder of the Old Testament, and finally with the New Testament.

The closer the concentric circle is to the center, i.e., the "text," the more important it is to helping one understand the meaning of the text. See the following diagram.[1]

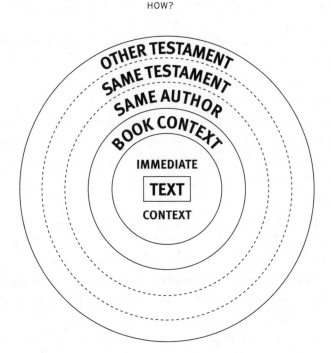

Approaching the text this way is essential because the biblical authors wrote their books with a particular overarching message in mind, and each chapter, section, paragraph, sentence, and word contributes to communicating that message. The major themes within a book are connected, with every passage contributing to the whole.

We need to ask how the passage functions and contributes to this message, beginning with its immediate context and then broadening concentrically beyond it, ultimately discovering how it contributes to the message of the entire Bible. This addresses the theological context of a passage, which will be discussed later.

The Literary Context

Given the fact that the Bible is literature, to understand what the biblical authors meant we need to examine how they chose to communicate. There are differences in how even the same writers wrote various passages.

For instance, in Exodus 14, Moses provides a moment-by-moment narrative of what happened when the Israelites crossed the Red Sea. However, in Exodus 15, he describes the same event with a song. Both descriptions communicate that God saved Israel and destroyed the Egyptians that day in the Red Sea. However, the way Moses communicated what happened in these two chapters is quite different.

Biblical scholars refer to the various types of literature in the Bible as *genres*. The word comes from French and literally means "form" or "kind." Therefore, when we consider the genre of a passage, we are asking what form of literary expression or structure the author employed. Why? Because the biblical authors wrote using literary forms people were familiar with in their context. They did this so that their audience would interpret what they wrote using the standards established in that particular literary form.[2]

The Bible encompasses a variety of genres, and scholars differ in how they categorize them. The authors of *Cracking Old Testament Codes* identify ten genres in the Old Testament: (1) narrative, (2) history, (3) law, (4) oracles of salvation, (5) announcements of judgment, (6) apocalyptic, (7) lament, (8) praise, (9) proverb, and (10) non-proverbial wisdom.

These ten genres belong to broader categories. The first three are considered types of prose, the next three are types of prophecy, the next two are types of poetry, and the last two are types of Wisdom Literature.[3]

Prose

The narrative genre in the Bible generally refers to stories. Stories are the most common way the ancients shared and passed down their histories from one generation to the next. It's important to realize that just because information is communicated in the form of a story does not imply that it's fictional. For example, even before my sons were old enough to understand, I began telling them stories about my father—all of which are true.

Similar to narrative is history or historical narrative. The differences between the two are subtle. Simply put, narrative is more like a story, and historical narrative is more like a report. This section loosely relates to both when addressing narrative.

There are three ways to think of narrative in the Old Testament: short narrative, extended narrative, and the grand narrative. The short narratives are the numerous stories within the Old Testament. Extended narrative refers to the numerous short narratives that are connected to one another to reveal God's dealings with his covenant people, Israel, both in the particular books as well as in the entirety of the Old Testament. The grand narrative is the story of the entire Bible that begins in Genesis 1:1 and concludes with Revelation 22:21. It's often referred to as the story of redemption or redemptive history. Every short narrative is part of an extended narrative, and every extended narrative is part of the grand narrative. Consequently, it's essential to look at how each of these types of narratives is connected to the other two or else we will not do justice to any of them.[4]

Given that more than 40 percent of the Old Testament is composed of narrative, it's important we keep certain principles in mind as we seek to interpret it.[5] Gordon Fee and Douglas Stuart provide ten principles for examining Old Testament narrative:

1. An Old Testament narrative usually does not directly teach a doctrine.
2. An Old Testament narrative usually illustrates a doctrine or doctrines taught propositionally elsewhere.

3. Narratives record what happened—not necessarily what should have happened or what ought to happen every time. Therefore, not every narrative has an individual identifiable moral application.

4. What people do in narratives is not necessarily a good example for us. Frequently, it is just the opposite.

5. Most of the characters in Old Testament narrative are far from perfect and their actions are too.

6. We are not always told at the end of a narrative whether what happened was good or bad. We are expected to be able to judge that on the basis of what God has taught us directly and categorically elsewhere in Scripture.

7. *All* narratives are selective and incomplete. Not all the relevant details are always given (cf. John 21:25). What does appear in the narrative is everything that the inspired author thought important for us to know.

8. Narratives are not written to answer all our theological questions. They have particular, specific, limited purposes and deal with certain explicit issues, leaving others to be dealt with elsewhere in other ways.

9. Narratives may teach either explicitly (by clearly stating something) or implicitly (by clearly implying something without actually stating it).

10. In the final analysis, God is the hero of all biblical narratives. In other words, the most important question about an Old Testament narrative is "What does this narrative reveal about God?"[6]

To determine where a narrative or story begins and ends, we should look for transitions in the text, like changes in locale, time, characters, and genre (recall the example of Exodus 14 and 15 moving from narrative to poetry).[7]

It is important to pay close attention to the introductions and conclusions to these narratives because they often provide clues to the author's purpose for including the story. Sometimes the author makes comments and summary statements about some aspect of the narrative to help the reader understand what is happening and what the point of the story is. Of course, many times the characters in the narrative are involved in dialogue. Given that it often appears we are not privy to every word that was said, it's important to notice what the author includes from the dialogue.

Another important feature of Semitic writing is repetition. The Old Testament authors often use repetition to emphasize aspects of their message. Stating something once is important, stating it twice is very important, and stating it three times means it is most important.

Whatever the author gives most attention to in the narrative is what we should focus on as well, and what the biblical author gives little or no attention to should be our clue that neither should we. As we investigate the meaning of the passage, we must always ask why the author chooses to include certain bits of information but not others. We should focus on what is in the text.

Law in the Old Testament is another type of prose. The Hebrew word *torah* is typically translated in our English Bibles as "law" or "instruction." The first section of the Hebrew canon is called the Torah. We often refer to it as the Pentateuch, "five scrolls/books," since the Torah consists of the first five books of the Old Testament. Of course, much of the Pentateuch is narrative and not legal material, but when we talk about the genre of law, we are talking about the actual sections of law in the Pentateuch.

The two types of law in the Old Testament are apodictic law and casuistic, or case, law. Apodictic laws are straightforward statements of what one must or must not do. For instance, the first of the Ten Commandments states, "You must not have any other god but me" (Exodus 20:3). It is an apodictic law, along with the rest of the Ten Commandments.

However, case laws address how certain situations should be dealt with. The basic structure is: In case this happens, then do this. For instance, Exodus 21:28 states, "*If* an ox gores a man or woman to death, [*then*] the ox must be stoned, and its flesh may not be eaten" (emphasis added).

It is helpful to consider God's purpose for giving the law according to the Scriptures. Both the Old and New Testaments provide reasons why God gave Israel his law.

1. The law reveals God's character. Deuteronomy 32:4 states, "Everything he does is just and fair. He is a faithful God who does no wrong; how just and upright he is!" And in Deuteronomy 4:8, Moses asked, "And what great nation has decrees and regulations as righteous and fair as this body of instructions that I am giving you today?" The God who is just, fair, and upright gives decrees and regulations that are righteous and fair. Paul wrote, "The law itself is holy, and its commands are holy and right and good" (Romans 7:12). As God alone is holy, right, and good, the law reveals and reflects God's character.

2. Therefore, the law is holy just as God is holy, and it reveals and defines what God means when he instructs his covenant people to be holy in Leviticus 19:2: "You must be holy because I, the LORD your God, am holy."

3. The law reveals sin (Romans 3:20).

4. The law provides a legal framework for the execution of God's justice (Ecclesiastes 12:13-14; Romans 3:19-20).

5. The law corrects those who will receive correction, and those who do so rejoice in it (Psalm 94:10-12).

6. The law is a source of joy to those who serve the Lord (Deuteronomy 4:1-5; 30:9-10; Joshua 1:8; Psalm 19:7-11; 119:33-40).

7. The law gives instruction for how one should think and live with complete love and devotion to God accompanied by a love for one's neighbor as for oneself (Psalm 119:9-12; Deuteronomy 6:5; Leviticus 19:18; Matthew 22:37-39).

8. The law provides a paradigm for how one should think and live (1 Timothy 5:17-18).

9. Obeying God's law provides a way of expressing love for God (Deuteronomy 30:16; John 14:15, 21).

10. God promised to write his law on the hearts of those with whom he makes a new covenant (Jeremiah 31:33).

11. The law was given to provide instruction, direction, and discipline for the people of God until Christ came to make his people right with God through faith in him (Galatians 2:16).

12. Obeying God's law provided a way for the people of God to point the nations to God (Deuteronomy 4:6-7).

In addition to the above reasons that God gave Israel the law, Timothy Valentino provides some general observations we should keep in mind about the law:

1. God's words to Israel just prior to his giving them the Ten Commandments indicate that God demonstrated his grace to Israel before he demanded obedience from Israel (Exodus 19:4; 20:2). Therefore, one may conclude that the law was not given to Israel to make them the people of God. God's covenant with Abraham had already secured that they were God's "own special treasure from among all the peoples on earth" (Exodus 19:5).

2. The Old Testament laws functioned as stipulations of God's covenant with Israel. They communicate God's expectations of Israel and what they may expect of him. They are to be obeyed by those who love him. These laws demonstrate both the *legal* and *relational* nature of this covenant.

3. God is the source of the law, given to Moses and to be taught by the priests. More importantly, it is the inspired, eternal, profitable Word of God, through which he reveals his values, priorities, and ways (Leviticus 10:11; Deuteronomy 10:12-13; 28:1; 33:10).

4. Obedience to God's law leads to a blessed life, but disobedience to it will result in destruction (Deuteronomy 4:1-5).

5. The law was characterized by the most impressive adjectives available to the Old Testament authors. Godly people had a positive relationship to God's law; they delighted in it (Psalm 19:7-14; 119:1-176).

6. The law was given to the people for their benefit not their detriment.

7. Many of the laws were meant to be paradigmatic. They provide examples with principles to apply to similar situations.

For example, as mentioned earlier, the law forbidding the muzzling of an ox as it treads the grain had broader applications to human laborers, according to later rabbis, as well as to pastors, according to Paul (1 Timothy 5:17-18).

8. The Old Testament law was not a means to salvation. Old Testament saints were saved like New Testament saints, by grace through faith in the Lord Jesus Christ. Along with every Old Testament believer, Abraham's faith in God and God's future provision for his salvation is what *saved* him. Old Testament believers looked forward to the person and work of the Lord Jesus Christ by faith just as we look back to him by faith (Genesis 15:1-6; John 8:56; Acts 4:11-12; Galatians 3:11; Romans 4:1-10, 16).[8]

So how should we as New Testament or new covenant believers approach a set of stipulations that were given to Israel in the old covenant, a covenant that is no more?

1. We need to remember the words of Jesus in Matthew 5:19, speaking about the law of Moses: "If you ignore the least commandment and teach others to do the same, you will be called the least in the Kingdom of Heaven. But anyone who obeys God's laws and teaches them will be called great in the Kingdom of Heaven." For this reason, we must not ignore the Old Testament law but instead understand that there is great blessing in teaching it.

2. Jesus gives full expression to the law and fulfills all its demands for righteousness (Matthew 5:17). Consequently, as New Testament believers we should recognize that Jesus has fulfilled the law by his death and resurrection. Jesus

is the ultimate authority and teacher of the law. We must therefore seek to understand it in light of him and the new covenant he inaugurated.

3. As Paul writes in 2 Timothy 3:16-17, "All Scripture is inspired by God and is useful to teach us what is true and to make us realize what is wrong in our lives. It corrects us when we are wrong and teaches us to do what is right. God uses it to prepare and equip his people to do every good work." As part of the Scripture, the law is inspired by God and profitable, so at the very least we should examine how its every ordinance reveals something about God's character, his values, and his will.

4. Given that we are New Covenant believers, we must view the law from a New Testament perspective, as exemplified in the writings of Paul and other New Testament authors.

5. Because God promised blessed lives to those who obey the law, we should ask what kind of life and society God envisioned for each individual and for Israel as a nation when they obeyed this law. And what did this law mean to its original recipients?

6. We must consider what concerns God articulated in a particular law for ancient Israel that are also concerns he has for believers today.

7. We should ask what kind of behavior the law promotes or seeks to prevent.

8. We should determine what moral principles are implied by a law and how they apply to us.

All these questions are essential to using Valentino's BETA method for teaching and preaching the Old Testament law:

- **B**ack-read the law from the New Testament context.
- **E**xamine the law in its Old Testament context.
- **T**heologize the law to its universal context.
- **A**pply the law to the present context.[9]

Undoubtedly, Old Testament scholars still find a few of the laws in the Pentateuch difficult to understand. But we are not ancient Israel and therefore are not under the old covenant. Still, there is much to learn in the Old Testament law about God and what he values for his people. Allan Moseley gives wonderful advice on how teachers in the church should endeavor to explain the law:

We are standing with the church looking *back* at the gift of the law. And we cannot look back without looking *through* the person and work of Jesus, the promised seed of Abraham who has come. In order to teach Old Testament law *as Christians,* we allow that perspective to affect our teaching. That means we will teach that God's gift of the law was good, but it was also temporary, preparatory, and pedagogical. It was temporary because God gave it with the foreknowledge that he would make it obsolete when he inaugurated the new covenant in Christ. It was preparatory because God used the law to demonstrate humanity's sinfulness and therefore our need for the Savior. It was pedagogical because God used the law to teach eternal principles such as the fact that sin leads to separation from God and death and God allows a substitutionary sacrifice to atone for sin. If indeed God was using the law to teach eternal principles and point to Christ, so can we.[10]

Prophecy

The prophetic literature comprises a substantial portion of the Old Testament. As we begin, it's worthwhile to make some general observations about the prophets of Israel.

1. They were messengers or ambassadors of the Lord. Sent by God with his authority, they represented him and delivered his proclamations to Israel. Therefore, some of the prophets are called "the man of God." This identifies them as men of godly character working in God's service.

2. The prophets came from various walks of life. Jonah was from Gath-hepher in the north; he lived during the time of the divided kingdoms of Israel and Judah, and he delivered a message of merciful, compassionate blessing to the evil King Jeroboam II (2 Kings 14:23-27). Amos also lived during the time of the divided kingdoms. Though he was a shepherd who also tended an orchard of sycamore figs (Amos 7:14), God called him to leave his home in Judah to deliver a message of God's judgment to Israel during Jeroboam's reign. Micah was from a small town in the south, and his contemporary, Isaiah, was part of the royal family in Jerusalem. Both Ezekiel and Jeremiah were from priestly families in Judah, but apparently only Ezekiel served as a priest.

3. Their books are basically anthologies, a collection of prophetic utterances often delivered by the prophet over a

period of time. Several of them proclaimed their various messages for a period of twenty to nearly fifty years.

4. "To prophesy does not primarily mean to foretell the future but rather to speak forth God's word in the present, a word that usually had as its content coming judgment or salvation."[11] The prophets were both foretellers and forthtellers, but they spent more time forthtelling than they did foretelling. Today, most of what the prophets foretold has already happened, either in the Old Testament context or with the first advent of Jesus Christ. Less than 2 percent of their prophecies were directly messianic, less than 5 percent describe the age of the new covenant, and less than one percent concern events that are still to come.[12]

The prophets spent much time urging the people of their day to respond to God's message at that time, a period that ranges from about 800–500 BC. Their primary audience was Israel as a whole or the kingdoms of Israel and Judah, and their basic objective was to exhort them to repent of their sin and return to their covenant relationship with the Lord.[13]

Recalling the blessings and curses promised in the covenant in Deuteronomy 28, the prophets expressed God's love for Israel while at same time warning the people of judgment to come because of their rebellion against God and the breaking of their covenant with him.

So while the Old Testament priests' main objective was to teach Israel how to *maintain* its covenant relationship with the Lord, the prophets' main objective was to encourage Israel to *return* to him and *restore* its relationship to him.

Many of the prophets follow a pattern of condemnation of sin, a declaration of judgment, an exhortation for repentance, and a proclamation of restoration as a result of God's salvation (it sounds a lot like the gospel).

There are three broad subcategories of prophetic utterances: salvation oracles, judgment oracles, and apocalyptic pronouncements. The salvation oracles focus on God's deliverance and restoration of his people. Micah 4 is an excellent example of this.

The judgment oracles focus on the first three parts of typical prophetic utterances. Sometimes the prophets deliver their message from the Lord in the form of a lawsuit where God is the prosecutor, judge, and executioner. It contains a summons, witnesses, testimony, the charges, the verdict, and then the sentencing. Micah 6 is an example of this type of oracle.

Among the judgment oracles is a subcategory called woe oracles, which are indications of God's judgment and declarations of imminent doom for the recipients. These oracles follow a simple pattern of a pronouncement of pending calamity, the details of it, and the reason for it. Amos delivered two consecutive woe oracles in 5:18-27 and 6:1-14. Isaiah uses the word *woe* six times between chapters 28 and 33, and Habakkuk pronounces woe oracles against the Babylonians in Habakkuk 2:6-20.

Apocalyptic pronouncements often include universal, cosmic, and calamitous language to describe God's judgment and subjugation of the nations followed by his universal reign over all his creation. Ezekiel 38–39 and Daniel 7–12 are examples of prophetic apocalyptic sections and language in the Old Testament.

Interpreting prophetic literature may seem daunting, but there are some basic questions to help us discover the meaning of the text.

1. *What is God revealing about himself in this prophetic message?* For example, a woe oracle may reveal God's anger toward people for their wickedness, but the fact that he sends his prophetic messenger to pronounce judgment demonstrates his desire to give them another opportunity to repent and turn back to him. We can see this in Jonah. Jonah only pronounced words of judgment on Nineveh, but when Nineveh heard God's prophet, the king along with all Nineveh's citizens repented. When God saw their repentance, he relented concerning the calamity he had threatened to bring upon them (Jonah 3:4-10).

2. *What is the prophet's main focus?* The prophets address several major themes, including the following:

    a. **Israel's love for Yahweh and its holiness through faithful obedience to his covenant:** Their love and devotion to Yahweh was to be demonstrated through obedience to his law and the rejection of all other gods. They were to worship and obey Yahweh alone and no other. Therefore, their idolatry was likened to unfaithfulness to one's spouse (e.g., Hosea's message). Going through the actions of doing what the law specifies is useless if doing what it says isn't accompanied by a heart truly devoted to God. Religious activities are no substitute for faithful obedience.

    b. **Love of neighbor:** As God had shown compassion to Israel when it was oppressed in Egypt, the people of God needed to show compassion to one another. Israel's lack of social concern for the needy was a major reason God gave for sending his people into exile. This was a significant focus of Amos's message.

c. **God's faithfulness to his covenants:** God is faithful to keep the promises he has made to his people Israel, both for ill and good. In Deuteronomy 28:14-68 and 29:15-29, God warns the people of the consequences of their unfaithfulness to his covenant with them. The prophets remind the people of these warnings and proclaim that God is about to do all he promised to do, including banishing them from their land, if they disobey his commandments and worship other gods. However, in Deuteronomy 30:1-10, God promises he will restore his people from exile and bless them. With regard to the Abrahamic covenant in particular, God promised he would curse those who mistreat God's covenant people. Several of the prophets, like Nahum and Obadiah for example, demonstrate that God is faithful to keep this promise.

d. **The Day of the Lord:** The Day of the Lord will be a day of punishment for the enemies of God and his people and a day of vindication for those who have remained faithful to the Lord. There is both a sense of near and far fulfillment in the prophets' messages concerning the Day of the Lord. Thus, some of the occurrences of God's judgment during Israel's day are just foretastes of the ultimate, universal Day of the Lord that is still to come.

e. **The Messiah:** As previously noted, the prophets anticipated the coming of the Messiah and provided some details (and sometimes only glimpses) about who he would be and what he would do.

3. *What is the fallen condition focus in the text?* We should put ourselves in the sandals of the original audience as much as possible and try to understand what the message meant to them.

   Bryan Chapell defines the Fallen Condition Focus (FCF) of a passage as "the mutual human condition that contemporary believers share with those for or by whom the text was written that requires the grace of the passage to manifest God's glory. . . . It simply needs to be an aspect or problem of the human condition that requires the instruction, admonition, and/or comfort of Scripture. . . . It is something wrong (though not necessarily a moral evil) that needs correction or encouragement from Scripture."[14]

   Nehemiah 4 provides an example of a wrong that the people of God were experiencing because they were doing what was right in rebuilding the wall of Jerusalem. The FCF in Nehemiah 4 is that when the people of God do his work, their enemies will oppose them. This truth is upheld in both Testaments (1 Timothy 3:6-7; 2 Thessalonians 3:2-5).

4. *So what?* We will address this question more thoroughly in a later discussion because it's one to ask of every passage of Scripture. But when we see the problem that a prophetic passage addresses, we must consider the Bible's answer to the problem not only in its immediate and surrounding context but especially through the lens of the New Testament and the person of Christ.

Poetry

A great deal of the Old Testament is written in Hebrew poetry. For instance, in the Pentateuch, Exodus 15 and Deuteronomy

32–33 are predominantly poetry. In the historical books, Judges 5, 1 Samuel 2:1-10; 2 Kings 19:21-28; and Nehemiah 9:5-38 are poetry.

Large sections of the prophetic literature also are poetry. For example, Micah, Habakkuk, Obadiah, and Nahum are 100 percent poetry. Zephaniah is 95 percent, Hosea is 94 percent, Isaiah is 82 percent, and Amos is 80 percent.[15]

So while we may think of the Psalms when contemplating poetry in the Old Testament, we must recognize that many biblical authors utilized this literary form in their writing.

There are important, sometimes difficult, characteristics to be aware of when thinking about Hebrew poetry in the Old Testament.

1. It is not like Western poetry in that it has very little rhyming.
2. It often contains little or no regularity in meter and rhythm.
3. Syntactically, it is the most difficult Hebrew in the Old Testament, making it sometimes very difficult to translate.
4. It is literary artistry. Consequently, no single rule prevails. In other words, some Hebrew poetry contains meter and rhythm or appears to follow a syntactical order.

Given these observations, there are other characteristics of Hebrew poetry that help as we study poetic passages. First, the basic unit of Hebrew poetry is the line. Lines are usually grouped as two or three to make a verse. Lines are to strophes in poetry what sentences are to paragraphs in prose. Just like writers put together sentences to form one idea in a paragraph, lines strung together form a strophe to communicate one main idea in poetry. And just like multiple paragraphs may form a single passage in prose, multiple strophes taken together will form a complete passage in poetry.

For instance, Psalm 119 contains twenty-two strophes, one for each letter of the Hebrew alphabet. Each strophe is made up of lines that are eight verses communicating something about God's law. One might say Psalm 119 provides the A to Z (or the aleph to tav in Hebrew) concerning the law of God. It is a complete song/ statement regarding the law of God. Each strophe provides one of the main ideas that, taken together, contribute to the overarching main idea of the entire poem or psalm, as in the case of Psalm 119.

In the Psalms, *selah*, which literally means "to lift up," sometimes separates strophes. Beware of saying *selah* means "stop and think about it." This has been popularized, but Hebrew scholarship has not substantiated this. It is possible *selah* is a musical notation meaning "pause," but it is just as possible it means to "lift" or raise the volume of the music or people's voices. The bottom line is that we do not know for sure. Therefore, we should not communicate that we do. After all, what passage of Scripture should we not pause and think about?

The main feature of Hebrew poetry is parallelism. Parallelism is the structuring of lines to exhibit patterns of literary symmetry and balance. These patterns may be exhibited through vocabulary, structure, ideas, and meaning. The biblical poets utilized several types of semantic, logical, and rhetorical parallelism to communicate their messages. Parallelism is the tool these writers used artistically to expand upon their subject matter and emphasize their main ideas.

Parallelism serves a variety of purposes, and there are several types utilized in the poetry of the biblical authors in the

Old Testament. It may provide intensification or specification of meaning.

For instance, Psalm 29:6 states, "He makes Lebanon's mountains skip like a calf; he makes Mount Hermon leap like a young wild ox." God not only makes Lebanon's mountains skip, but he causes the grandest mountain of all, Mount Hermon, to leap. The second line is more specific and grander in scale. It's what scholars call synonymous parallelism, where "Lebanon's mountains" corresponds to "Mount Hermon," and "skip like a calf" corresponds to "leap like a young wild ox." However, one should note that synonymous does not mean exactly the same in Hebrew poetry. Instead, it means they convey a similar idea that is usually grander in the second line.

Antithetic parallelism contrasts two ideas. For example, Psalm 90:6 states, "In the morning it blooms and flourishes, but by evening it is dry and withered."

In synthetic parallelism, the lines following line one add something to its meaning. For instance, Psalm 25:9 says, "He leads the humble in doing right, teaching them his way." Here, David uses the second line to explain how the Lord leads the humble in doing right. He does so by teaching them his way.

Another common type of parallelism is climactic or step parallelism, where there is the repetition of similar lines that lead to a climactic statement. The repetition builds up the emphasis. Note Psalm 29:1-2:

> Honor the LORD, you heavenly beings;
>> honor the LORD for his glory and strength.
> Honor the LORD for the glory of his name.
>> Worship the LORD in the splendor of his
>> holiness.

While synonymous parallelism is the most common type in the Hebrew poetry, it is chiastic parallelism that seems to get the most attention among students of the Scriptures. Chiastic or inverted parallelism is when the lines in the first half build to a climactic center, and the lines in the second half correspond to the lines in the first half in reversed order. It is something like A-B-C-D-C-B-A. Whatever is in the center is the emphasis of the passage.

For instance, note the chiastic structure David used to confess his sin against God in Psalm 51:4: "Against you, and you alone, have I sinned; I have done what is evil in your sight." Note how "against you" and "in your sight" correspond to one another. However, "I have sinned" and "I have done what is evil" is at the heart or center, literally, as the focus of his confession.

The biblical authors utilized each type of parallelism to articulate their message. Therefore, it is important to become familiar with the various types when seeking to understand how and what the author wants to communicate.[16]

Given the Psalms are poetry, it is also fitting to mention various types of psalms that were the songs and hymns for Israel's worship.

Laments are cries for help and expressions of grief from those who have put their hope in God. They are the cries of his trusting children. The issue may be concerning the nation or the individual.

Imprecatory psalms express the people's desire for God to uphold justice for his covenant people, to vindicate his righteousness, and to put an end to wickedness. They should not be understood as expressions of personal vendetta. Instead, they anticipate God's final judgment on the nations.

Psalms of thanksgiving reflect on a past distress and on God's deliverance. They conclude with words of praise and thanksgiving to God for what he has done. Some psalms are entirely corporate hymns of praise by the people of God.

There are wisdom psalms, which are instructional or revolve around a motif that comes from the Wisdom Literature.

The people sang psalms of ascent as they made their pilgrimages to the Temple to worship.

Messianic or royal psalms emphasize the anointed king.

To communicate their messages, the psalmists employ several artistic literary forms of expression, such as personification, metaphor, simile, detailed imagery, hyperbole, wordplays, analogy, and irony.

Wisdom Literature

Derek Kidner provides one of the best statements concerning the purpose of the Wisdom Literature in the Bible: "Its function in Scripture is to put godliness into working clothes; to name business and society as spheres in which we are to acquit ourselves with credit to our Lord, and in which we are to look for his training."[17]

Whereas most of the Bible focuses on the consequences of the Fall and God's restoration of humanity's relationship to him through the story of redemption, the Wisdom Literature focuses on how to navigate life with God's perspective in this fallen world.

The Old Testament writers understood the varied uses of the word *wisdom, hōkmah*, in their culture. It could refer to being skilled in a particular trade. An expert craftsman might literally be said to be a "wise," meaning one who is highly skilled, such as Bezalel and Oholiab and those who joined them in constructing the Tabernacle (Exodus 36:2). Wisdom in the Old Testament may refer to mental capacity or logic as in 1 Kings 2:6. Also, there is the wisdom or way of thinking of the world that leads to destruction (Isaiah 47:10-11).

But primarily, wisdom in the Old Testament should be understood to be theological. God is the source of it and the goal of it. To speak of God's wisdom is to recognize he is morally right (righteous) and functionally right. God knows what is right and does what is right in the right way, at the right time, and to the right extent. Therefore, one who is wise knows God and seeks to live according to God's wisdom.

There are several themes in the Wisdom Literature.

1. The sages understood that God created the universe with order and that it operates according to that order. Therefore, according to them, sin or foolishness is to live life in rebellion against God's created order.
2. This order is teachable and learnable, and living according to it results in a life of satisfaction. The proverbs, for example, provide solid guidelines to this end.
3. All of life comes as a gift from God, and the only things with eternal value are those done by God and unto God. Any pursuits for wisdom, pleasure, or wealth apart from God as the focus of one's life are futile.
4. God's ways are often difficult to discern, but he is sovereign and in control of all things, while at the same time life is out of human control.
5. Wise people trust God and his sovereign will for their lives.
6. People should enjoy their spouse and the family, food, and work God gives them.
7. Recognizing time is a gift from God, wise people have a proper perspective of their mortality and are mindful of how they spend their time on earth.
8. Wise people learn from the mistakes of others.
9. Wise people recognize obedience is more important to God than their religious expressions of devotion.

10. Wise people live circumspectly, "fearing God" and obeying his Word, realizing that they will give an account to him for how they lived their lives.

The "fear of the Lord" or "fearing God" is a major theme in Old Testament Wisdom Literature, as well as a common expression throughout both the Old and New Testaments. The "fear of the LORD is the foundation of true knowledge" (Proverbs 1:7), and "Fear of the LORD is the foundation of wisdom. Knowledge of the Holy One results in good judgment" (Proverbs 9:10).

What is the fear of the Lord? Many today espouse that there is no element of fear in "fearing God." However, Paul wrote to the Philippian believers that they should work out their salvation with "fear" and "trembling" (Philippians 2:12, NIV).

There is an element of fear in "fearing God," but it is not a fear that God is against us. For Christians, the fear of the Lord is a consuming, deep-seated reverence and awe for God that causes believers to hate evil and instead desire to honor him at all costs and avoid his loving discipline. It involves attentiveness, trust, submission, obedience, consideration, wonder, admiration, worship, and love, inspired by his eternal attributes and authority.

To summarize, the Wisdom Literature should be understood as a guide to how God intends for his people to live —keeping him at the center of their lives—in a fallen world. Lasting satisfaction in life is enjoyed only by those who live according to these precepts. Consequently, when studying or teaching Wisdom Literature, we should approach it with this perspective.

11

What?

WHAT DOES THE PASSAGE MEAN? is really the question we've been trying to answer all along. As we've already seen, in chapter 2, the question of *what* may refer to the theological context of the passage. It might also refer to the *words* the authors used in their writing—on the biblical languages, more specifically. Thus, that will be our focus here.

In his 2021 faculty address at The Southern Baptist Theological Seminary, professor Robert Plummer enumerated reasons for why those who teach the Bible should utilize the biblical languages in their studies.

1. **Biblical languages are essential because we value the Word of God.** Plummer states, "God inspired the underlying Hebrew, Greek, and Aramaic words of Scripture and

if the Scripture is the ultimate authority for our lives and ministries, when disagreements happen and push comes to shove, we must ultimately appeal to those Hebrew, Greek, and Aramaic grammatical constructions."[1]

2. **The biblical languages are important because we value teaching and preaching that is both biblical and original, fresh, relevant.** Those who listen to you preach God's Word need to hear what God has taught you in your studies.

3. **Biblical languages are essential because we have limited time.** A working knowledge of the biblical languages will save time by connecting us directly to the text and to the best resources. My ability to work with Hebrew has allowed me to go directly to the best lexicons to understand how Hebrew and Aramaic words are used in the Old Testament. To grasp the full meaning, we must also understand how words are used in both their immediate and surrounding contexts.

4. **The biblical languages are essential because they are the "sap in the tree" that nourishes the other disciplines.** In other words, the discussion of theological, ethical, and cultural concerns based on God's Word must be rooted in the words that make up God's Word, and these words were written in Hebrew, Aramaic, and Greek.

5. **The biblical languages are essential to know because of the trust people place in those of us who teach God's Word.** They are looking to us to expound the precious Word of God. It is truly a matter of spiritual life or death. We must do all we can to understand it so that we may accurately and faithfully teach it to others.[2]

Today, given the sustained work of biblical scholars and scholarly publications, made accessible by the latest technology and the internet, there are many great tools to help both beginners and veterans study the biblical languages and utilize them in preparation for teaching the biblical text.[3]

Another important aspect to addressing what words the biblical authors used is to determine which words in the passage are essential to understanding the meaning. On which words does the passage depend?

There are several indicators that a word may be a key word.

1. Look for theological and unusual expressions or words that appear to be necessary for communicating the meaning of the text.
2. Look for repeated words. The more often a word appears in a passage, the more important its meaning. The Old Testament authors repeated words to emphasize them.
3. Look for words that are difficult to understand. Doing word studies may help you understand them better.

After selecting the word, look it up in Hebrew. A free and easy way to do this is to use Biblehub.com, where you can look up a verse. Once there, click on "Strong's" toward the top of the page. This will take you to every word in Hebrew in the verse and its various meanings (known as its semantic range) in the Old Testament according to the Strong's Lexicon.

Usage is everything. How the biblical authors used a word to communicate meaning is what we need to know. You should notice that under the Hebrew word, Strong's indicates what stem and part of speech it is. This is especially important for verbs because the stems provide the nuanced usages of verbs, and there is a difference between a perfect, an imperfect, a participle, an infinitive, and an imperative.

If you want to look at every occurrence of the Hebrew word in the Old Testament (and you do), then click on the transliteration next to the Hebrew word. There you will see every verse in which the word is located in the Old Testament and how three or four Bible versions translate it in each verse.

Finally, go back to the text you are studying and look at its immediate context to determine what usage of the word in the Old Testament best fits the usage of the word in the passage.

If you have the funds, Logos or Accordance Bible software will also serve you well—and there may be others as well. Some software packages offer a multitude of other resources and commentaries to help with studying a passage. Given these resources, there's no reason not to do a thorough word study on the key words in a passage.

12

Why?

WE HAVE ADDRESSED THE IMPORTANCE of examining the immediate and surrounding context of a passage in its Old Testament theological context. But in this section, we need to address why this passage was included in the grand narrative of the story of redemption.

All the Scriptures, taken together, lead to the person and work of Jesus Christ. This does not mean every single passage speaks specifically about the Messiah, but it means that every passage is part of the story that Jesus completes.

Christopher J. H. Wright astutely observes, "Not only must we see the Old Testament as a story that makes sense in the light of Jesus but also we have to understand Jesus in the light of the story that goes before. Jesus came into the world because of all that had happened in the story so far. That is why we need to read, understand, teach, and preach from the Old Testament. We do it for Christ's sake. It is his story."[1]

However, not every part of the Bible appears to have been written like a story, especially some sections in the Old Testament like the law. So it might be better to understand that all of the texts in the Bible are essential parts to the grand narrative of the story of redemption, as seen in six stages.

Stage 1: Creation (Genesis 1–2).

Stage 2: The Fall, when sin entered the human race through Adam and Eve (Genesis 3–11).

Stage 3: The Promise. It begins with the covenant God made with Abraham to use him and his seed to be a blessing to the nations, to be the instrument God uses to bring salvation to the world. It anticipates the coming person and work of Jesus, the Messiah (Genesis 12—Malachi).

Stage 4: The Gospel. In the Gospels, we see that Jesus has come and accomplished through his life, death, burial, resurrection, and ascension everything that is necessary for salvation (Matthew—John).

Stage 5: The Mission. Before Jesus ascended to his Father, he commanded his followers to join him in his mission by carrying out the Great Commission to every nation (this mission is to be carried out in the period of time between Jesus' ascension and his second coming).

Stage 6: The New Creation. This is the time when Jesus will return to purge and restore creation with a new heaven and earth, where he will reign with his redeemed people.[2]

When we study and teach the Old Testament, we are looking at what happened in Stages 1–3 from the perspective of Stage 5 (where we now live), in light of Stage 4, and anticipating the coming of Stage 6.

So when we look at a passage from the Old Testament, the proper question is not "Where is Jesus in this passage?" as if the Bible were a *Where's Waldo?* book. The important question is "What essential role does this passage play in anticipation of the person and work of the Lord Jesus Christ?"

For instance, the Old Testament narratives contain many accounts of the failures of Israel's and Judah's kings. They typically do not mention the Messiah; but when we view them through the lens of Christ, we recognize that he is the only king from the seed of Abraham and David who could fulfill the messianic expectation of a righteous king who will execute justice and establish peace as he rules over the nations (Isaiah 2:2-4; 9:7; 11:1-16; Revelation 17:14; 19:16).

In his thought-provoking work, *Preaching Christ from the Old Testament*, Sidney Greidanus suggests seven possible ways that an Old Testament passage can fit into the grand biblical narrative that culminates in Jesus Christ.

1. *By redemptive-historical progression:* following the progression of redemptive history as it moves forward from the text's historical setting to Jesus' first or second coming

2. *By promise-fulfillment:* showing that the promise of a coming Messiah was fulfilled in the person and work of the Lord Jesus Christ

3. *By typology:* moving from an Old Testament type prefiguring Jesus to Jesus himself. A genuine type must be (a) historical; (b) theocentric—a discernable action of God, rather

than the actions of human beings; (c) it must exhibit historical and theological correspondence between the proposed type and Jesus; and (d) Jesus must depict something much greater than the limited type—sometimes called escalation.

4. *By analogy:* noting the similarity between the teaching of the text and that of Jesus

5. *By longitudinal themes:* tracing a theme of the text throughout the Old Testament to Jesus in the New Testament

6. *By New Testament references:* moving to New Testament quotations of or allusions to the Old Testament in the preaching text of the New Testament or to Jesus' similar teachings

7. *By contrast:* noting the contrast between the message of the Old Testament and that of Jesus. I would add that it is important to highlight the contrast between the portrayal of human depravity in the Old Testament with the righteousness of Christ and the flaws of humanity with the perfection of Christ.[3]

Addressing these concerns should help answer our question regarding the role a passage plays in the story of redemption. No doubt there will be those who object to this approach.

I had a professor who objected to any attempt to understand the Old Testament through the lens of the New Testament. He said, "If you preach an Old Testament passage and sound like a Jewish rabbi when you are done, then you have done a good job. One must not jump too quickly to Christ."

But I am a Christian, not a Jewish rabbi. Therefore, I cannot help but see the entirety of the Scriptures through the lens of

Christ. I am compelled to do so in light of the examples provided for us in the New Testament.

Of course, we begin our investigation of an Old Testament passage addressing its historical-cultural context, its literary context, and its theological context in the Old Testament. However, we must also address the redemptive historical context. What's more, while we must be careful not to jump too quickly to Christ, we must at the same time recognize that all the Scriptures are ultimately fulfilled in him. Consequently, we must be just as careful to avoid making the grave error of ignoring him.

13

So What?

INVESTIGATING A PASSAGE TO UNDERSTAND its meaning is incomplete if we fail to ask, "So what?"

The Bible is more than a textbook with interesting information. It is the story of redemption, God's call through the work of the Holy Spirit to salvation by grace alone through faith alone in Jesus Christ alone. What's more, in his Word God reveals his demand for our love, worship, devotion, and faithful obedience to him as his children, saved by his grace.

For this reason, God speaking to us through the Scripture necessitates our response. Remember the words of James,

> But don't just listen to God's word. You must do what it says. Otherwise, you are only fooling yourselves. For if you listen to the word and don't obey, it is like glancing

at your face in a mirror. You see yourself, walk away, and
forget what you look like. But if you look carefully into
the perfect law that sets you free, and if you do what it
says and don't forget what you heard, then God will bless
you for doing it.

JAMES 1:22-25

Therefore, addressing the relevance and applicability of the
text is paramount. Having a correct understanding of a passage is
necessary before applying it.

Bible teachers do not need to make the Scriptures relevant.
Given that Scripture is the eternal Word of God, our mandate
is to show people *how* it is relevant, necessary, and applicable to
them today.

This is where Bryan Chapell's instruction to look for the Fallen
Condition Focus of a passage can be beneficial. To discover the
FCF, Chapell recommends asking three successive questions:

1. What does the text say?
2. What concern(s) did the text address (in its context)?
3. What do listeners spiritually share in common with those
   for (or about) whom it was written or the one by whom it
   was written?[1]

This entails looking at how the biblical author wanted the
original audience to apply the meaning of the text. How does the
meaning of the text in their day intersect with us today? Once
the FCF is recognized, then asking proper questions of application
will naturally follow.

One of the best resources for learning how to apply the
Scripture is Daniel M. Doriani's *Putting the Truth to Work: The*

Theory and Practice of Biblical Application. Doriani suggests four essential questions to ask when applying a text.

1. What should I do? That is, what is my *duty*? *Duty* is about needing to know what the Bible teaches us to do in a particular situation. Does the text provide an example to follow? Does it depict behavior we must shun? What changes to our actions and ongoing activities need to be made to bring our behavior and habits in line with the will of God?

2. Who should I be? That is, how can I become the person or obtain the *character* that lets me do what is right? *Character* is about who we are in Christ and how we may become more like him.

3. To what causes should we devote our life energy? That is, what *goals* should we pursue? *Goals* are about what should be the priorities in one's life and how one should set out to pursue these godly ends.

4. How can we distinguish truth from error? That is, how can we gain *discernment*? *Discernment* is about resisting what is false and clinging to what is true according to the Word of God. What changes do we need to make in our beliefs or thinking to bring them in line with the Scriptures? What is wisdom according to the Scriptures and how can one gain it from God within the community of faith, the church?[2]

Since the preacher's responsibility is to apply the text, all the answers to these questions must spring from the biblical text. The questions aren't to be used as a springboard to apply the text to one's hobbyhorse, that is one's own preoccupation or favorite topic.

If there is no analogy or correspondence between what the biblical author actually says in the text and the application we make, then we are ignoring the text instead of applying it. Placing oneself above the Scriptures demonstrates a low view of the Scriptures.

When applying the Scriptures, we must simultaneously keep two truths in mind. First, Paul wrote to Titus that Jesus "gave his life to free us from every kind of sin, to cleanse us, and to make us his very own people, totally committed to doing good deeds" (Titus 2:14). Paul also instructed the believers in Philippi to "work hard to show the results of your salvation, obeying God with deep reverence and fear" (Philippians 2:12). So we must be "totally committed" and "work hard" to obey and apply God's Word to fulfill Jesus' purpose for us and to demonstrate that we are believers.

At the same time, you must remember that "God is working in you, giving you the desire and the power to do what pleases him" (Philippians 2:13). God has given us the indwelling Holy Spirit to produce his fruit in us so that we may live according to the Spirit and no longer do what our "sinful nature craves." We must "follow the Spirit's leading in every part of our lives" (Galatians 5:16, 22-23, 25). To summarize, we must devotedly do everything we can to apply God's Word, while trusting God to guide and empower us to do so.

PART III

EFFECTIVE PRESENTATION

THE FOLLOWING IS ADVICE ON HOW TO deliver your sermon or lesson effectively. Having done a thorough investigation of the text, it's time to prepare to present it. This section doesn't contain extensive information on the subject, but it does hopefully provide some direction that is tried and true.

Of course, we also need to ask for God's help in this endeavor. In particular, we need to ask God to help us teach his Word so that those who hear will learn it and apply it. Teaching assumes learning. If those who hear us have failed to learn, then we haven't really taught.

Assuming you've selected a passage, there are important steps to take to put all the preparation work into a format that will communicate the main message.

Sidney Greidanus provides an approach that takes into consideration all the answers to the questions you've asked while thoroughly investigating a passage.

1. Select a textual unit with an eye to congregational needs.
2. Read and reread the text in its literary context.
3. Outline the structure of the text.
4. Interpret the text in its own historical setting.
5. Formulate the text's theme and goal.
6. Understand the message in the contexts of canon and redemptive history.
7. Formulate the sermon theme and goal.
8. Select a suitable sermon form.
9. Prepare the sermon outline.
10. Write the sermon in oral style.[1]

Outline

Many of the concerns in Greidanus's approach have already been addressed (e.g., literary context, historical-cultural context, redemptive history, understanding the text through the lens of the New Testament and the person and work of Jesus Christ). But there are a few issues still to address.

First, how does one formulate an outline of the text? An outline is important because it will help to recognize the structure, flow, and logic of the passage. Remember the passage is written to communicate truth. An outline helps to see how the author did so. This will benefit both teachers and learners, and we are all learners. We begin by looking for major divisions in the passage. What main idea connects them? Whatever idea interconnects the parts of a passage will be the main point of the passage.

For example, in Nehemiah 5, there are structurally three sections connected by one main concern. The first section is verses 1-5, which recount the allegations of some of the people of Judah against their brothers for not helping them but instead taking advantage of them in a difficult situation. In verses 6-13, Nehemiah responds to the people's complaints and confronts those who had failed to help and had taken advantage of the needy. Finally, verses 14-19 relate how Nehemiah personally showed compassion to his people during the difficult times. Each section speaks to the subject of helping those within their community who were in need.

1. Nehemiah listened to the concerns of the people in need (verses 1-5).
2. Nehemiah resolved the problem by making sure the people in need were being cared for and not being taken advantage of by others (verses 6-13).
3. Nehemiah personally did what he could to help those in need (verses 14-19).

Once the main points of the outline are understood, look at each main section to see how it is developed and write down the statements or ideas for each major point. For instance, in verses 1-5, there are three complaints in verses 1-2, verse 3, and verses 4-5 respectively. These are the supporting ideas for the first major point that "Nehemiah listened to the concerns of the people in need (verses 1-5)."

For each major point, make observations of the supporting ideas, arguments, or statements within that section of verses. Now we have the following:

1. Nehemiah listened to the concerns of the people in need (verses 1-5).

a. Complaint one (verses 1-2). Some of the Jews were unwilling to share food with fellow Jews who needed food.

b. Complaint two (verse 3). People were having to mortgage their homes to get grain because of a famine.

c. Complaint three (verses 4-5). People were borrowing money at interest and selling their properties and their children into servitude to their fellow Jews because of the economic situation.

Main Idea

Second, write down a declarative statement of the main point or idea of the passage.

Here is a declarative statement of the main idea of Nehemiah 5: Instead of taking advantage of those in need, the people of God must take care of one another, especially during difficult times. This declarative statement is what Greidanus calls the text's theme. The sermon's theme needs to correspond to the text's theme.

However, another way of understanding Nehemiah 5 is within its surrounding context of chapters 4 and 6. These chapters indicate how opponents to the rebuilding of the wall of Jerusalem tried to stop its construction. Therefore, Nehemiah 5 should also be understood to show how Nehemiah had to deal with numerous obstacles, caused by both outsiders and his own people, in order to accomplish the work that God had called him to do. So the specific issues in Nehemiah 5 were part of a bigger issue: opposition to the people of God doing God's work. In this instance, the sins of the uncaring people who were taking advantage of the needy became a potential obstacle to the rebuilding of the wall.

For practical reasons, such as time constraints, the teacher will need to decide what to focus on the most, but the rule of thumb is: "The main things are the plain things and plain things are the main things." Focus on the main things in the passage.

Introductions

The introduction is important to every sermon or lesson. What are its goals?

1. To engage the audience and gain its interest in what you are about to teach.
2. To inform the audience of the passage's main idea.
3. To inform the audience of the importance and relevance of the main idea.
4. To preview what is going to be taught.

For instance, a number of the psalms have the words "A maskil" in their introductions. A maskil is associated with teaching, and the psalms were ancient Israel's songs.

Psalms 42–43 were originally one psalm. Psalm 42:1 (NIV) indicates it is "a maskil of the Sons of Korah." What is its main idea? Psalm 42–43 provides enlightenment to believers whose perspective on life has been darkened by feelings of alienation and despair, who are experiencing discouragement, disappointment, adversity, disillusionment, broken dreams, and confusion.

With that said, here is an example introduction:

"Think of a song you learned somewhere along the way that was used to teach you something. Share the title of that song with someone sitting near you." (Give them a moment to do so, but don't wait for everyone to get done. Keep it moving.)

"I asked my wife this question, and she thought of 'The Alphabet Song.' Did any of you think of that? I thought of Kenny Rogers' 'The Gambler.' I'm not sure why this song came to mind. Maybe it's because my name is Betts.

"When we look to Psalm 42–43, it states it is a 'maskil,' a song that was written to teach us something. These chapters are a song that was written to teach us what we should do when we're feeling alone, in despair, or oppressed" (the three points of my outline for the text).

I'm sure you could improve it, but this introduction does everything I want it to do. It immediately engages the audience and gets them thinking about what I'm going to say by having them engage with others about the subject without even realizing it. What could this possibly have to do with what this speaker is about to preach? The main topic is a maskil, and songs used for instruction are all familiar to us. Its relevance comes to bear because everyone has at one time or another experienced a feeling of loneliness, despair, or oppression. Also, I have laid out for them my overall outline of what I'm about to say:

1. Alienation: When you feel alone, remember God is with you (42:1-5).
2. Desperation: When you feel despair, remember God will help you (42:6-11).
3. Vindication: When you feel oppressed, remember God will vindicate you (43:1-5).

By the way, in case you're wondering, the outline divides with the phrase "hope in God" in 42:5, 42:11, and 43:5. Using repetitive phrases is a common way the biblical authors used to divide the sections in a psalm or prophetic passage.

Lloyd John Ogilvie provides a list of suggested ways to introduce a sermon or lesson:

1. A personal story from my own life pilgrimage, followed by application of the biblical text and statement of purpose

2. A real-life story that gets to the essence of what you feel called to preach, followed by the purpose of the message and the biblical text

3. An anecdote or parable from contemporary life or history that exposes the central issue of the biblical text. Then state the purpose and press on with the thesis and points of the body of thought.

4. A direct statement of the biblical text and what it promises for our contemporary life

5. A sympathetic reference to a need expressed by many in the congregation and how the biblical text offers a promise to meet that need

6. The dramatic retelling of the story line of a biblical account with "you are there" intensity and sensitivity. State the purpose and, with empathy, hold out the hope that what happened then can happen now.

7. The straightforward statement of a contemporary problem, moving to the biblical text and the idea that the truth therein is the solution to that problem

8. Asking questions that get to the core of a human need. These "Do you ever . . ." questions should be followed by

an "Of course, we all do" kind of empathy, and then the statement of how God can meet the need and how this message will help explain what he is ready to do.

9. A clearly stated paragraph of the essential truth which the entire message will elucidate. Then break down into the points to be covered and press on.

10. Recounting of a current news item that is on people's minds, dilating the contemporary focus for the biblical text to be preached. This opens the way to show how the Bible speaks today, answers our "why" questions, and meets our deepest needs.[2]

Explanation, Illustration, Application

One simple approach to teaching and preaching is *explanation*, *illustration*, and *application*. This is not original with me, but I learned it more than forty years ago, and I cannot remember the source.[3]

Each major point of the outline should support the overall main point of the passage. Therefore, use each major point of the outline as a jumping-off point to explain that section of the text, incorporating the subpoints to do so. This is where all the hard work of investigation comes together.

The explanation obviously involves telling your audience what the text means, but an illustration paints a mental picture to *show them* what it means. This can be very powerful in clarifying the meaning of the text. An effective illustration will capture people's attention, give them time to consider what the text means, and help them remember its meaning with a concrete mental picture of it. People tend to remember illustrations more than explanations. For this reason, it is imperative that the illustration communicates the meaning of the text, complementing the explanation of the text.

Charles Spurgeon is known as "The Prince of Preachers," and few preachers have been as adept as he was with illustrations. Spurgeon used an illustration to explain the importance of illustrations to preaching and teaching and to give advice on how to use them.

He compared illustrations to windows on a house. The purpose of windows is to bring light into a house. Likewise, illustrations should cast light on the meaning of the text. Just as windows greatly enhance the "agreeableness of a habitation," illustrations make a sermon or lesson more interesting and pleasurable. Also, as a house should not have too many windows, a message or study must not have too many illustrations. What's more, they must not be so prominent that they distract from the point they are supposed to illustrate. Illustrations are best when they naturally spring from the subject at hand. Finally, keep them simple and in good taste.[4]

Michael Kruger's "Five Major Pitfalls to Avoid" in sermon illustrations is also beneficial, and they correspond to Spurgeon's advice.

1. **Avoid giving an illustration too soon.** Be sure you have adequately explained the text before illustrating it.
2. **Avoid using too many illustrations.** Usually one effective illustration per major point is plenty.
3. **Avoid offering only one kind of illustration.** Stories, metaphors, similes, and word pictures can all be effective.
4. **Avoid getting illustrations from the same type of source all the time.** For instance, you may enjoy movies, but not everyone else does. If every illustration comes from

a movie, even others who enjoy movies will begin to get annoyed by it. Use a variety of sources and choose illustrations that virtually everyone in your audience can relate to.

5. **Avoid using illustrations that are so over-the-top that they distract from the point they are supposed to be illustrating.**[5]

Along with these warnings, be careful to avoid talking too much about your family or yourself. Certainly these can be great sources for powerful illustrations, and there is a place for them. But most preachers' kids prefer that their parents keep them out of their sermons. There is enough pressure on them already to be different from the rest of the kids, and often they already stand out and are judged for their good behavior or poor behavior. Also, don't embarrass family members, and as a general rule, one should not use the pulpit to try to make oneself look good. It's ultimately about pointing people to Christ, not to us.

How to apply a passage has already been addressed, but there is one more thing to keep in mind when communicating an application to the text. As with illustrations, the targets or subjects of life applications of the text should vary. Passages have one meaning, but they may be applied in a number of ways and in various settings. Consider the variety of backgrounds and lives represented in the audience when making applications. Not everyone is single, not everyone is married, not everyone has children, not everyone is fifty years old, not everyone is male, not everyone is female, etc. Like illustrations, applications need to apply to as many people as possible and be varied enough so that, over the course of time, no one is left out.

Petition

As we began the process in prayer, we need to offer our petitions to the Lord after we have delivered the study or message. Through his prophet Isaiah, the Lord declared, "The rain and snow come down from the heavens and stay on the ground to water the earth. They cause the grain to grow, producing seed for the farmer and bread for the hungry. It is the same with my word. I send it out, and it always produces fruit. It will accomplish all I want it to, and it will prosper everywhere I send it" (Isaiah 55:10-11).

Trusting God, we need to pray that his Word will be received by those who hear it, that it will take root and bear fruit in their lives, and that it will accomplish everything God wills it to accomplish for his glory and the building up of his church.

Trusting through Trials

Sample Sermon Outline

Genesis 43:1–45:28

HERE IS A SERMON OUTLINE BY BLAKE SHUECRAFT, using Genesis 43:1–45:28, to help you apply Sydney Greidanus's ten-step model for preaching Christ in the Old Testament.

1. Select a textual unit with an eye to congregational needs.
   - Genesis 43:1–45:28

2. Read and reread the text in its literary context.

3. Outline the structure of the text.
   - Setting
     - Go buy food in Egypt (43:2).
   - Occasioning incidents
     - The famine was severe in the land (43:1).
   - Complications
     - We cannot go back without Benjamin (43:3-5).
     - Judah promises himself if Benjamin does not return (43:9).

- • The brothers bow before Joseph (43:26-28).

- • The cup is placed in Benjamin's sack (44:2).

- • The cup is found in Benjamin's sack (44:12).

- • The brothers feel guilt (44:16).

- • Judah gives a speech (44:18-34).

- Conflict climax

  - • Judah offers himself in place of Benjamin (44:33).

- Resolution

  - • Joseph could not control himself, and he cried (45:1-2).

  - • I am Joseph (45:3)!

  - • The brothers are shocked (45:3).

  - • Do not be distressed (45:5).

  - • God sent me before you to preserve life (45:5).

  - • God sent me before you to preserve a remnant (45:7).

  - • It was not you who sent me here but God (45:8).

  - • Dwell in the land of Goshen (45:10).

  - • Pharaoh is pleased (45:16).

  - • Pharaoh gives them the best of the land of Egypt (45:18).

- Outcome

  - • Joseph is alive, and I will see him before I die (45:28).

4. Interpret the text in its own historical setting.

   - Literary interpretation (chiastic/inverted structure)

     - • The scenes are arranged as a chiasm:

A. Jacob sends his sons back to Egypt (43:1-14).

  B. Arrival in Egypt: the brothers meet Joseph's steward (43:15-25).

    C. Joseph and his brothers eat together (43:26-34).

      D. The brothers are arrested (44:1-13).

    C'. Joseph reveals himself to his brothers (44:14–45:15).

  B'. Departure from Egypt: the brothers meet Pharaoh (45:16-24).

A'. The sons report to Jacob what happened (45:25-28).

- Historical interpretation
  - Moses is showing Israel that they can trust in God's providence. God will continue to be faithful to Israel and even use the difficult circumstances to fulfill his promises.
- Theocentric interpretation
  - Although this story primarily focuses on Joseph and his brothers, God providentially carries out his plan. This idea is brought directly to the reader when Joseph reveals himself to his brothers and declares that God, not them, sent him to Egypt.

5. Formulate the text's theme and goal.
   - Theme: God sovereignly used the sinfulness of Joseph's brothers to send Joseph to Egypt so that he may preserve a remnant for Israel.
   - Goal: The author is calling Israel to trust in God. God, in his sovereignty, can use sinful actions to fulfill his plan of preserving a remnant for Israel.

6. Understand the message in the contexts of canon and redemptive history.

   - God promised Abraham that he would be a great nation and that all of the earth would be blessed through him (Genesis 12:2). There was a severe famine in the land that could have killed Jacob's family. However, God, in his sovereignty, through the wickedness of Joseph's brothers, sent Joseph to Egypt ahead of Israel so that he might become a ruler and save Israel from the famine. Israel settled in the land of Egypt, was fruitful and multiplied greatly (Genesis 47:27), and became a great nation. Through Joseph, God was fulfilling his promises to Abraham that would ultimately be fulfilled through Jesus Christ.

7. Formulate the sermon theme and goal.

   - Theme: God sovereignly uses suffering to accomplish his plan and purposes.
   - Goal: Hearers must trust God through suffering.

8. Select a suitable sermon form.

   - Redemptive-historical progression in narrative
     - Personal history (Joseph)
     - National history (Israel)
     - Redemptive history (Christ)

9. Prepare the sermon outline.

Introduction: God is redeeming, restoring, and saving a people by his grace and for his glory.

I. Individual history: Joseph (Genesis 37:1–41:57)

A. Unpredictable circumstance: sold

i. Joseph is sold into slavery.

a. Jacob loved Joseph more than any of his other sons, but his brothers hated him because of Jacob's favoritism (37:3-4).

b. Joseph has two dreams revealing that he will rise to power and that his brothers will bow before him (37:5-11).

c. The brothers devise a plan to kill Joseph when they see him coming from a distance, but they end up selling him into slavery at the advice of Judah (37:18-28).

d. Joseph's brothers deceive Jacob into believing that Joseph is dead (37:31-33).

ii. Joseph is brought into Potiphar's house. The Lord was with Joseph and caused him to succeed at everything he did (39:1-6).

a. When Potiphar saw that Joseph was successful, he put Joseph in charge of everything he owned, and the Lord blessed Potiphar's house for Joseph's sake (39:3-6).

b. Joseph refused the advances of Potiphar's wife and was falsely accused and thrown into prison (39:7-20).

   iii. The warden put Joseph in charge of all of the
        prisoners. The Lord was with Joseph (39:21-23).

       a. Pharaoh sends the cupbearer and the baker to
          prison for their offense against him, and Joseph
          is appointed over them (40:1-4).

       b. The cupbearer and the baker have troubling dreams,
          and Joseph interprets them. The cupbearer will
          be restored to his position, but the baker will be
          executed (40:5-19).

       c. The dreams are fulfilled by Pharaoh three days
          later, just as Joseph interpreted. Joseph tells the
          cupbearer to remember him and mention his name
          to Pharoah, but Joseph is forgotten (40:20-23).

   iv. Joseph has been betrayed, sold for the price of a
        slave, falsely accused, abandoned, and left for dead in
        prison.

B. Unexpected outcome: savior

   i. Joseph becomes the savior of the people.

       a. Pharaoh has two dreams. He is distraught, but he
          can find no one to interpret his dreams (41:1-8).

       b. The cupbearer remembers Joseph and tells Pharoah.
          Joseph is brought before Pharoah, interprets Pharaoh's
          dreams, explains that his (i.e., Joseph's) interpretation
          comes from God, and then proposes a plan (41:9-36).

       c. Pharoah recognizes that God is with Joseph, so he
          gives Joseph authority over all his kingdom; only
          the king, Pharoah, will be greater than Joseph
          (41:37-43).

    d. Joseph implements the plan given by God: he stores up food for the seven good years, and when the famine comes, people from all over the earth travel to Egypt to buy food so that they may live (41:46-57).

II. National history: Israel (Genesis 42:1–45:28)

A. Unpredictable circumstance: famine

    i. The first journey: Jacob's family is suffering because of the famine, so Jacob sends his sons to Egypt to buy food. All go except Benjamin (42:1-5).

    a. Joseph tests his brothers and accuses them of being spies. He puts them in prison and then holds Simeon captive while they go home to get Benjamin to prove that they are honest men (42:6-26).

    b. The brothers discover the money in their sacks. The brothers feel guilty about how they treated Joseph and believe that God is doing this to them because of their sin (42:27-28).

    c. They return home to Egypt to explain to Jacob what has happened. However, Jacob refuses to send Benjamin back with them. Jacob is afraid that Benjamin will also die (42:29-38).

    ii. The second journey: The famine in the land is so severe that the brothers must return to Egypt to buy more food (43:1-2).

    a. After a passionate plea to Jacob, Judah receives permission to take Benjamin to Egypt with them to buy more food (43:3-15).

     b. In a tense encounter with Joseph's steward, the brothers explain that the money was in their sacks, only to find that the steward responds graciously to them (43:16-30).

     c. Joseph has a meal prepared for the brothers. He seats them according to birth order and gives Benjamin five times the portions of the others (43:31-34).

  iii. The final test: Joseph puts the silver cup in Benjamin's sack and accuses the brothers of stealing (44:1-6).

     a. The brothers respond by pledging the life of the one who stole the cup (44:7-13).

     b. The brothers confess that God is punishing them for their sins against their brother (44:14-17).

     c. Judah pleas on behalf of his brother and offers himself in place of Benjamin (44:18-34).

B. Unexpected outcome: feast

  i. Joseph could no longer control himself, and he revealed himself to his brothers and assured them that it was God's sovereign plan to send him there to save the family (45:1-8).

     a. Joseph's brothers are dismayed that their brother is alive (45:3).

     b. Joseph reassures them three times that God, not them, sent him there (45:4-8).

  ii. Joseph instructs his brothers to go to their father and tell him that Joseph is alive, that he is a ruler in the land, and that they must bring Jacob and the family to Egypt in order to be provided for. Then Joseph and his brothers are reconciled (45:9-15).

iii. Jacob is amazed that his beloved son, Joseph, is not dead but alive and highly exalted (45:25-28).

III. Redemptive history: Christ (Romans 1:18-32; 3:5-26)

A. Predictable circumstance: rejected

i. All of us face the same circumstance: sin. All of us have sinned and fallen short of the glory of God (Romans 3:23).

ii. As a result, all of us have rejected God. We desire our ways over God's ways and are separated from God because we have rejected him.

iii. Although we sinned against God and deserve wrath for our sins, God is gracious to us and promises that there is one who will come from the seed of the woman and take care of the curse of sin.

iv. This story is much bigger than Joseph. It anticipates the one who is to come, Jesus.

B. Unexpected outcome: redeemer

i. Jesus is our redeemer.

ii. Joseph had to suffer so that Israel might live, and Christ had to suffer so that you might live.

iii. Trust in Jesus as your redeemer.

Conclusion: You must trust God through suffering.

> i. Despite Joseph's suffering, he trusted in God.
>
> ii. Outside of Christ we are all hopeless and will face never-ending suffering separated from God.
>
> iii. God is saying, "Trust me."

10. Write the sermon in oral style.

Notes

CHAPTER 1: THE OLD TESTAMENT IS THE WORD OF GOD

1. Rein Bos, *We Have Heard That God Is with You: Preaching the Old Testament* (Grand Rapids, MI: Eerdmans, 2008), 7–8.
2. See, for example, Andy Stanley, *Irresistible: Reclaiming the New That Jesus Unleashed for the World* (Grand Rapids, MI: Zondervan, 2020).
3. Robert L. Plummer, *40 Questions about Interpreting the Bible* (Grand Rapids, MI: Kregel, 2010), 37–45.
4. Plummer, *40 Questions*, 41–44.
5. Guy Prentiss Waters, *What Is the Bible?: Basics of the Faith*, ed. Sean Michael Lucas (Phillipsburg, NJ: P&R Publishing, 2013), 15.
6. Waters, *What Is the Bible?*, 16.

CHAPTER 2: THE OLD TESTAMENT IS GOD'S REVELATION OF HIMSELF

1. The spellings on this list are an approximation of how the words are pronounced in Hebrew. Some English Bible translations attempt to do this, but others do not. See Marilyn Hickey, *The Names of God* (Whitaker House, 2009) and Christopher D. Hudson, *100 Names of God Daily Devotional* (Rose, 2015) for helpful studies and devotions concerning the meanings and significance of the names of God in the Bible.
2. T. Desmond Alexander, *Exodus*, Apollos Old Testament Commentary, ed. David W. Baker and Gordon J. Wenham, vol. 2 (London: Apollos, 2017), 89.
3. Ludwig Koehler et al., *The Hebrew and Aramaic Lexicon of the Old Testament* (Leiden: E. J. Brill, 1994–2000), 1072.
4. Mark F. Rooker, *Leviticus*, The New American Commentary, vol. 3A (Nashville: Broadman & Holman, 2000), 251.

5. See, for example, A. W. Pink, *The Attributes of God*; A. W. Tozer, *The Knowledge of the Holy*; J. I. Packer, *Knowing God*; Peter Toon, *God Here and Now*.

6. Keith H. Essex, "The Abrahamic Covenant," *The Master's Seminary Journal* 10, no. 2 (Fall 1999): 212.

7. Peter J. Gentry and Stephen J. Wellum, *God's Kingdom through God's Covenants* (Wheaton, IL: Crossway, 2015), 185.

8. Eugene H. Merrill, *Kingdom of Priests: A History of Old Testament Israel*, 2nd ed. (Grand Rapids, MI: Baker Academic, 2008), 204–205.

CHAPTER 3: THE OLD TESTAMENT ANTICIPATES JESUS

1. Alec Motyer, *Look to the Rock* (Grand Rapids, MI: Kregel, 2004), 22.

2. G. K. Beale and D. A. Carson, eds., "Introduction," in *Commentary on the New Testament Use of the Old Testament* (Grand Rapids, MI: Baker Academic, 2007), xxvii.

3. Duane Garrett, *The Problem of the Old Testament: Hermeneutical, Schematic & Theological Approaches* (Downers Grove, IL: IVP Academic, 2020), 236.

4. Christopher J. H. Wright, *Knowing Jesus Through the Old Testament* (Downers Grove, IL: IVP Academic, 1992), 150.

5. Andrew G. M. Hamilton, *How to Preach the Prophets for All Their Worth: A Hermeneutical, Homiletical, and Theological Guide to Unleash the Power of the Prophets* (Eugene, OR: Wipf & Stock, 2022), 6–7.

6. Wright, *Knowing Jesus*, 145.

CHAPTER 4: THE OLD TESTAMENT LAYS THE FOUNDATION FOR THE NEW TESTAMENT

1. For a work dedicated to addressing the New Testament authors' use of the Old Testament, see G. K. Beale and D. A. Carson, eds., *Commentary on the New Testament Use of the Old Testament* (Grand Rapids, MI: Baker Academic, 2007).

2. Craig L. Blomberg, "Matthew," in *Commentary on the New Testament Use of the Old Testament*, 2.

3. R. T. France, *Matthew: An Introduction and Commentary*, Tyndale New Testament Commentaries, vol. 1 (Downers Grove, IL: IVP Academic, 1985), 45.

4. France, *Matthew: An Introduction*, 41.

5. Rikk E. Watts, "Mark," in *Commentary on the New Testament Use of the Old Testament*, 111.

6. David W. Pao and Eckhard J. Schnabel, "Luke," in *Commentary on the New Testament Use of the Old Testament*, 251.

7. Andreas J. Köstenberger, "John," in *Commentary on the New Testament Use of the Old Testament*, np.

8. Robert D. Bergen, *1, 2 Samuel*, The New American Commentary, vol. 7 (Nashville, TN: Broadman & Holman, 1996), 337.

9. Bergen, *1, 2 Samuel*, 337–338.

10. G. J. Steyn, *Septuagint Quotations in the Context of the Petrine and Pauline Speeches of the Acta Apostolorum*, Contributions to Biblical Exegesis and Theology, vol. 12 (Kampen, the Netherlands: Kok Pharos, 1995), 26–31; Richard N. Longenecker, *Biblical Exegesis in the Apostolic Period*, 2nd ed. (Grand Rapids, MI: Eerdmans, 1999), 69–71.

11. I. Howard Marshall, "Acts," in *Commentary on the New Testament Use of the Old Testament*, 513.

12. George H. Guthrie, "Hebrews," in *Commentary on the New Testament Use of the Old Testament*, 919.

13. Douglas J. Moo, *James: An Introduction and Commentary*, Tyndale New Testament Commentaries, ed. Eckhard J. Schnabel, 2nd ed., vol. 16 (Downers Grove, IL: IVP Academic, 2015), 51.

14. Merrill F. Unger, *Unger's Bible Handbook* (Chicago: Moody, 1982), 783.

15. D. A. Carson, "1 Peter," in *Commentary on the New Testament Use of the Old Testament*, 1015.

16. Mark A. Seifrid, "Romans," in *Commentary on the New Testament Use of the Old Testament*, 607.

17. Seifrid, "Romans," 607–608.

18. Moisés Silva, "Galatians," in *Commentary on the New Testament Use of the Old Testament*, 786.

19. Silva, "Galatians."

20. Silva, "Galatians."

21. Frank S. Thielman, "Ephesians," in *Commentary on the New Testament Use of the Old Testament*.

22. Moisés Silva, "Philippians"; G. K. Beale, "Colossians,"; Jeffrey A. D. Weima, "1–2 Thessalonians"; Philip H. Towner, "1–2 Timothy and Titus," in *Commentary on the New Testament Use of the Old Testament*.

CHAPTER 5: THE OLD TESTAMENT GIVES WISDOM UNTO SALVATION

1. Josephus, *Antiquities of the Jews*, 10.210.

2. Thomas D. Lea and Hayne P. Griffin, *1, 2 Timothy, Titus*, The New American Commentary, vol. 34 (Nashville: Broadman & Holman, 1992), 234.

CHAPTER 6: THE OLD TESTAMENT PROVIDES INSTRUCTION FOR NEW TESTAMENT BELIEVERS

1. Thomas R. Schreiner, *Romans*, Baker Exegetical Commentary on the New Testament, vol. 6 (Grand Rapids, MI: Baker, 1998), 748.

2. "Bava Metzia 88b," *The William Davidson Talmud* (Koren-Steinsaltz), accessed May 21, 2022, https://www.sefaria.org/Bava_Metzia.88b.2?ven=William _Davidson_Edition_-_English&vhe=Wikisource_Talmud_Bavli&lang=bi.

3. George W. Knight, *The Pastoral Epistles: A Commentary on the Greek Text*, New International Greek Testament Commentary (Grand Rapids, MI: Eerdmans, 1992), 449.

4. T. J. Betts, *Nehemiah: A Pastoral and Exegetical Commentary* (Bellingham, WA: Lexham Press, 2020), 64.

5. Philip Towner, *1–2 Timothy & Titus*, The IVP New Testament Commentary Series, vol. 14 (Downers Grove, IL: IVP Academic, 1994), 200–201.

PART II: PREPARING TO TEACH THE OLD TESTAMENT

1. Walter C. Kaiser Jr., *Preaching and Teaching from the Old Testament: A Guide for the Church* (Grand Rapids, MI: Baker Academic, 2003), 54.

2. For example, in the Tyndale Old Testament Commentary on the book of Jonah, T. Desmond Alexander's note says, "In the MT this section is numbered 2:1–11; 1:17 in the English translations is the first verse of chapter 2 in the Hebrew text." He divides his comments on the passage between Jonah 1:4-16 and 1:17-2:10 accordingly. See, David W. Baker, T. Desmond Alexander, and Bruce K. Waltke, *Obadiah, Jonah and Micah: An Introduction and Commentary*, Tyndale Old Testament Commentaries, ed. Donald J. Wiseman, vol. 26 (Downers Grove, IL: IVP Academic, 1988).

3. Alistair Begg, *The Main Things* (blog), September 9, 2015, https://blog .truthforlife.org/the-main-things.

4. Howard G. Hendricks and William D. Hendricks, *Living by the Book* (Chicago: Moody, 1991), 197.

5. Robert H. Stein, *A Basic Guide to Interpreting the Bible: Playing by the Rules*, 2nd ed. (Grand Rapids, MI: Baker Academic, 2011), 16.

6. The Tyndale Old Testament Commentary (TOTC) is an excellent example of a solid expositional commentary series. The Bible Speaks Today series is also very good.

CHAPTER 8: WHEN?

1. Gordon D. Fee and Douglas Stuart, *How to Read the Bible for All Its Worth*, 2nd ed. (Grand Rapids, MI: Zondervan, 1993), 22.

2. J. Scott Duvall and J. Daniel Hays, *Grasping God's Word: A Hands-On Approach to Reading, Interpreting, and Applying the Bible*, 3rd ed. (Grand Rapids, MI: Zondervan, 2012), 118.

3. Duvall and Hays, *Grasping God's Word*, 117.
4. Scholars are split on dating the time of the Exodus, an Early Date View vs. a Later Date View. Given my understanding of Exodus 1:11; 1 Kings 6:1; 1 Chronicles 6:33-37; and Judges 11:26, I believe the Early Date View makes the most sense. You may check out my discussion of some of the issues in "Dating the Exodus," *The Southern Baptist Journal of Theology* 12, no. 3 (Fall 2008), https://sbts-wordpress-uploads.s3.amazonaws.com /equip/uploads/2015/10/Betts-SBJT-Fall-08-3.pdf (accessed June 1, 2022).
5. For an exceptional evangelical resource on the history of Israel in the Old Testament, see Eugene H. Merrill, *Kingdom of Priests: A History of Old Testament Israel*, 2nd ed. (Grand Rapids, MI: Baker Academic, 2008).
6. Chronology of the Hebrew Kingdoms created by Dr. George Martin, professor of Christian missions and world religions at The Southern Baptist Theological Seminary, Louisville, KY. For a helpful chart titled "A Timeline of Biblical History: Major Events from Creation to the Completion of the New Testament," see https://alwaysbeready.com/wp -content/uploads/2020/04/Timeline-of-Biblical-History-by-Charlie -Campbell-AlwaysBeReady-dot-com.pdf.

CHAPTER 9: WHERE?

1. Howard F. Vos, *Wycliffe Historical Geography of Bible Lands*, rev. ed. (Peabody, MA: Hendrickson, 2003), vii.
2. Paul H. Wright, *Holman Illustrated Guide to Biblical Geography: Reading the Land* (Nashville, TN: Holman Bible, 2020), 7.
3. Wright, *Holman Illustrated Guide*, 12.

CHAPTER 10: HOW?

1. Circles of Context diagram is copyright © 2017 Orange Lutheran High School, Orange, CA. Used by permission.
2. Robert H. Stein, *A Basic Guide to Interpreting the Bible: Playing by the Rules*, 2nd ed., (Grand Rapids, MI: Baker Academic, 2011), 70.
3. D. Brent Sandy and Ronald L. Giese, Jr., *Cracking Old Testament Codes: A Guide to Interpreting the Literary Genres of the Old Testament* (Nashville, TN: Broadman & Holman, 1995), vii–viii.
4. Gordon D. Fee and Douglas Stuart, *How to Read the Bible for All Its Worth*, 2nd ed. (Grand Rapids, MI: Zondervan, 1993), 79–80.
5. Stein, *A Basic Guide to Interpreting the Bible*, 79.
6. Fee and Stuart, *How to Read the Bible for All Its Worth*, 83–84.
7. Allan Moseley, *From the Study to the Pulpit: An 8-Step Method for Preaching and Teaching the Old Testament* (Wooster, OH: Weaver Book, 2017), 54.

8. Timothy R. Valentino, "Using Expository Preaching to Promote a Christian Understanding of Old Testament Law at Fleetwood Bible Church, Fleetwood, Pennsylvania," (DMin. project, The Southern Baptist Theological Seminary, 2009).
9. Valentino, "Using Expository Preaching," 65.
10. Allan Moseley, *From the Study to the Pulpit*, 94.
11. Fee and Stuart, *How to Read the Bible for All Its Worth*, 240.
12. Fee and Stuart, *How to Read the Bible for All Its Worth*, 166.
13. Some might argue that Jonah's audience was Nineveh, but the book records only five words in Hebrew that Jonah spoke to the people of Nineveh. The message of the book of Jonah is the entire book of Jonah, and its audience was the people of Israel as part of the Book of the Twelve.
14. Bryan Chapell, "The Fallen Condition Focus and the Purpose of the Sermon," Preaching.com, https://www.preaching.com/articles/the-fallen-condition-focus-and-the-purpose-of-the-sermon.
15. Most English translations indicate these passages are poetry by changing the way they indent their left margins. Note the differences between Exodus 14 and 15.
16. For a helpful explanation of the type of parallelism used in the Old Testament see Andreas J. Köstenberger and Richard D. Patterson, *For the Love of God's Word: An Introduction to Biblical Interpretation* (Grand Rapids, MI: Kregel Academic, 2015), 124–141.
17. Derek Kidner, *Proverbs: An Introduction and Commentary*, Tyndale Old Testament Commentaries, vol. 17 (Downers Grove, IL: IVP Academic, 1964), 33.

CHAPTER 11: WHAT?
1. Robert L. Plummer, "The Necessity of Biblical Languages in Ministerial Training," annual faculty address at The Southern Baptist Theological Seminary, September 22, 2021, *The Southern Baptist Journal of Theology* 25, no. 3 (Fall 2021), 199.
2. Adapted from Plummer, "The Necessity of Biblical Languages," 198–204.
3. One of the best websites for Hebrew is Daily Dose of Hebrew, overseen by my dear friend and colleague Adam Howell, at https://dailydoseofhebrew.com/. For Aramaic, check out Daily Dose of Aramaic at https://dailydoseofaramaic.com/, and for Greek see Daily Dose of Greek, which is overseen by another dear friend and colleague, Robert L. Plummer, at https://dailydoseofgreek.com/.

CHAPTER 12: WHY?
1. Christopher J. H. Wright, *How to Preach & Teach the Old Testament for All Its Worth* (Grand Rapids, MI: Zondervan, 2016), 28.

2. Wright, *How to Preach & Teach the Old Testament*, 35–36.
3. Adapted from Sidney Greidanus, *Preaching Christ from the Old Testament: A Contemporary Hermeneutical Method* (Grand Rapids, MI: Eerdmans, 1999), 227–277.

CHAPTER 13: SO WHAT?

1. Bryan Chapell, "The Fallen Condition Focus and the Purpose of the Sermon," Preaching.com, https://www.preaching.com/articles/the-fallen -condition-focus-and-the-purpose-of-the-sermon.
2. Daniel M. Doriani, *Putting the Truth to Work: The Theory and Practice of Biblical Application* (Phillipsburg, NJ: P&R Publishing, 2001), 98–102.

PART III: EFFECTIVE PRESENTATION

1. Sidney Greidanus, *Preaching Christ from the Old Testament*, 279–292. Blake Shuecraft, a pastor at First Baptist Mayfield, Kentucky, graciously shared his application of Greidanus's method for a sermon he preached from Genesis 43:1–45:28. It is located in the appendix.
2. Lloyd John Ogilvie, "Introducing the Sermon," Preaching.com, https:// www.preaching.com/articles/introducing-the-sermon.
3. Wayne McDill advocates this approach adding "argumentation" to the mix. See Wayne McDill, "How to Balance Four Critical Elements of Preaching," Lifeway, January 1, 2014, https://www.lifeway.com/en/articles /pastor-balance-four-critical-elements-preaching.
4. Charles H. Spurgeon, *Second Series of Lectures to My Students: Being Addresses Delivered to the Students of the Pastors' College, Metropolitan Tabernacle*, 13–26, https://www.princeofpreachers.org/uploads/4/8/6/5/48652749/chs _student_lectures_vol_2.pdf.
5. Adapted from Michael J. Kruger, "Do Your Sermon Illustrations Help or Hurt? Five Major Pitfalls to Avoid," *Canon Fodder* (blog), April 20, 2015, https://www.michaeljkruger.com/do-your-sermon-illustrations-help-or -hurt-five-major-pitfalls-to-avoid.

About the Author

T. J. BETTS is an Ohio native and pastored churches in Ohio and Indiana for more than fourteen years before joining the faculty at Southern Seminary, where he now serves as professor of Old Testament interpretation. He authored *Ezekiel the Priest: A Custodian of Tora*; *Amos: An Ordinary Man with an Extraordinary Message*; *Nehemiah: A Pastoral & Exegetical Commentary*; and *40 Days in Psalms 1–50*. Along with other publications, he writes for Lifeway's Explore the Bible study series and is a regular contributor to the men's devotional *Stand Firm*. He received his BS from Wright State University and his MDiv and PhD from Southern Seminary. Dr. Betts and his wife, Ann, live in southern Indiana, where they enjoy their children and grandchildren.